GRAY

A STORY OF LOSS

ERICA STONE

*To my husband and family.
Thank you for loving me and
for patiently waiting on me to navigate the wilderness.*

*To Osseh.
You are my safe place, my brother.
Always.*

*And to Beth.
I would have never finished this book without our trip to Rosemary.
You've changed my life.*

I dedicate this book to all of you.

CONTENTS

The Blow	8
The Report	14
The Haze	27
Before the Day that Changed Everything	34
Waiting Games	44
The Plan	55
When Good News Becomes Bad News	66
The Facts	76
The Burial	84
Crossing the Water	90
Blow by Blow	97
Night Only Lasts So Long	110
The Compound	121
The Bench	131
Righting the Wrong	138
Run Child Run	145
The Choice	154
Hotel 510	162
Modern Day Miracle	171
2010	181
The Resurrection	188
Homecoming	195
The Afterlife	199
POSTFACE	205

Erica Stone

Your silence gives consent.
—Plato

PREFACE

I'm going to attempt to tell you a story. A story that's true. A story that avoids spiritual dogma and clichés. I'm going to try to stay away from all the words we say to one another when our world crumbles.

In God's timing.
It must not have been in the plan.
It must not be God's will.

We say these things, even though we know the words carry little weight when our world is falling apart around us.

I'm going to tell you about miracles and tragedies. I'm going to be honest about how my brain breaks down and why I now question all things.

1.

THE BLOW
2011

I have been one acquainted with the night.
—Robert Frost, *Acquainted with the Night*

She was dead.

Buried in the red clay dirt, on the side of a highway, on the outskirts of Freetown, cast out like yesterday's trash.

I tried to absorb that fact. It was a bitter pill filled with the cold hard truth. A truth I didn't want to believe. I'd been forced to swallow it, although I tried to refuse it, as though pretending it wasn't happening would somehow take my reality and make it all a dream.

I swallowed the pill and told myself the truth. Again.

She. Was. Dead.

The words shook my insides. I could feel the breakdown coming.

I sat there inside the room cold as stone, forcing the woman across the desk to make eye contact with me. I wrapped my fingers around the arms of the chair as though holding on tighter would keep me from pouring out. I refused to cry in front of the others. I was afraid of the river I might create. I was afraid of the stories they would tell. I knew deep down, it was my fault. It was my fault that Adama was dead. But I wanted it to be her fault, the woman on the other side of the desk. God how I wanted to cast blame and look for someone else to nail to a cross for it. After all, I was the "White Savior," wasn't I? That's what they like to call us modern-day, white American women intent on saving the world. It makes me sick to think I actually was that person back then.

In my mind, the corrupt government was at fault. The evil people who held Adama hostage and used her like a chess piece in a game the rest of the world calls child exploitation, they were at fault. How could it possibly be my fault? Wasn't I the good guy in all of this? It's easy to mask truth by casting shadow and spewing blame, but in the end, today, seven years later, I know the truth. Her death was on me. I never said it out loud. I never carried the cross where the rest of the world could see me, but underneath my fight for justice swelled a river of grief that told me it was on me. I just couldn't admit it to anyone else. So, I put my head down and while I bled out on the inside, I fought. I fought the way I should have while she was alive. If only. If only I had fought for Adama like I have for so many others. It would all be different.

I can remember the day so well.

I packed my backpack that morning and found myself tucking granola bars into the side pockets, making sure not to forget the cheerios.

She loved cheerios.

I can still remember how Adama's hands would catch the leftover pieces that never made it to her mouth, soggy and sticking to her fingers like glue. She would try so hard to keep from dropping any. She would stuff as many as she possibly could into that tiny little mouth of hers. Most would end up stuck between her fingers or spilled into her lap or my lap. And believe me, I welcomed the mess.

So much time would pass between my visits. I would use the cheerios to lure her back into my arms in case she forgot me. She was such a timid child. She was afraid of almost everything, and people she didn't know threw her straight over the edge. I never wanted to be the one to make her cry. So I always showed up armed and ready to coerce her into loving me until she remembered who I was again. I still buy cheerios. Even though most of my kids won't eat them. It just feels right to have them sitting in the pantry, waiting for her.

The last time I saw Adama it wasn't the visit I had hoped for. Ina, the woman who was keeping her from me, basically holding her hostage in that hellhole disguised as an orphanage, refused to let me actually hold her or spend time with her that day.

Ina believed that if she held Adama over my head, dangled her in front of my face, reminding me that I was living without her, I would crack and give her what she wanted. The pay-off. The $10,000. I won't lie, there are days I wish I had caved and done what most people would consider the unthinkable. Days I wish I'd paid her whatever she wanted. After all, was a pay-off really wrong if a child's life was hanging in the balance? If it had been my first-born son, I wonder if I'd have done it. Actually, there is no question. I would have paid the bribe. If Jordan had been taken from me and held for ransom, I would have paid the bribe. Any mother would. So why was I so afraid of doing whatever it took for Adama? There is no easy answer for my behavior at the time.

My heart would scream that the right thing for me to do was to rescue her from these monsters. The right thing was to fight for her until my knuckles bled. At the same time, my head was telling me different. The right thing was clear: Stand up against bribery and tribal alliances. There was no choice. I could *not* cave. If I did, I would be like the rest of them, the people who choose to sit silent in the face of adversity. The people who choose to shrink when the right thing is the hardest thing. The right thing was supporting the law, the law few people ever followed. Right and wrong couldn't exist in the same space. In order to do right by the law, I had to do something wrong. And that's where I stayed — in the uncertainty, in the gray, not making a move, afraid of the fallout.

Years before, when all my work in Sierra Leone began, before I knew anything about anything, I assumed it would all be so easy. Children were struggling. We had resources to help them. Bottom line. That should be the end of it. But nothing was ever simple. The work you choose to do in countries like Sierra Leone comes with a price. The price I paid, and am still paying today, was steep.

On the last day I ever saw Adama, I was allowed to bring the center food and water, and I could watch her play from a distance. But Ina wouldn't let me go near her. It was clear that until we came to an agreement, I couldn't touch Adama or even let her know I was there. So that's what I did. I stood back in the corner of the room and watched as the children lined up for lunch. At first, I couldn't find her, and then I realized she wasn't even in the room. I asked a caregiver about her. She stared at me as though she didn't even know who Adama was. She disappeared for a bit to try to find her, and then before I knew it she came back with my little baby girl in tow. Adama lethargically found her way into the room, dragging behind the caregiver, rubbing her eyes. Snot was running down her face, and she struggled with a deep cough that told me she wasn't well. She was wearing a giant pageant style dress. It was a cornflower blue. God it was ugly. Who knows where she got it. It was several sizes too big with the shoulders hanging off both sides. The ruffles were bigger than she was. I almost laughed out loud at the sight, except that a cry stuck in my throat instead.

Adama struggled to wake up. I struggled to not run to her. As she took her spot on the front row the ache in my throat grew. I couldn't swallow for fear I would break down and cry an ocean. Oh, how I wanted to hold her. But I couldn't. I wanted to run. But I couldn't. I wanted to scream and demand my child be returned to me. But I didn't. I stood frozen, afraid that a wrong move could keep me from her forever. So, I stayed silent. A decision I regret with everything inside of me. I had no idea that day would be my last day with her. If I'd known, I would have fought harder. If I'd known, I would have scooped her up. I would have run, and I would have refused to turn her over. I would have called in the troops and every news station. I would have told anyone who would listen. I would have made sure the world knew what was happening to my child. She was a prisoner in her own country, but I didn't know.

I didn't know.

2.

THE REPORT
2011

What's done cannot be undone. —William Shakespeare, *Macbeth*

My mind kept drifting back to that day. The day I didn't know, the last day I saw her. I was so anxious to replace that memory with a happy one. I couldn't wait to get my hands on her. I wanted to wrap my arms around her and smother her in the love I had overflowing from my insides. There is nothing worse than dreaming about your child and not being able to hold her, not knowing who is tucking her in, and if she's okay. It's pure torture, especially when the people caring for her are people you cannot trust.

♦ ♦ ♦

You may wonder how I was separated from Adama in the first place. Several years before this particular day, we had opened an orphanage. During that same time, we were trying to adopt Adama. I had traveled to Sierra Leone with a team of women who helped us launch the center, including my mother-in-law who came to stay with Adama during the day while I worked. Our attorney said we could take physical custody of Adama upon arrival. Our court date would be scheduled as soon as we landed in-country. Unfortunately, it didn't go down like that. Once we arrived, we learned that our attorney had left the country without telling us and turned our case over to a junior attorney with little adoption experience. I knew in that moment we might be in trouble. We had no legal coverage, and that was very important. Things moved from bad to worse. Ina began acting very strangely. She wasn't showing up to our meetings. When she did, she struggled turning Adama over to me. She began to make excuses for why she wasn't showing up and then went MIA. Before I could piece together what was happening, a man began calling me. He worked at the orphanage with Ina. He said they had demands and expectations of me. They had made the decision they would not turn Adama over to me until we "negotiated" further.

I reported the situation to Social Welfare, claiming that I believed the employees at Ina's orphanage had intentions to bribe me. I received *zero* support. The people at Social Welfare scoffed and told me the "timing" was all wrong, regardless of whether a bribery attempt had taken place. The choice was clear. I could either open an orphanage or adopt Adama. With the recent trafficking scandals in-country, Social Welfare couldn't — wouldn't — support me in both. Never mind the fact that we had a legal adoption supported by the law in process, the concern was that opening an orphanage while simultaneously adopting a child would appear as though I intended to move children in and out of the country. That I was trafficking children.

I felt at that time I had no choice. The decision had been made. I had women who left their families to assist in opening our orphanage. They were back at the hotel waiting on me. I couldn't just send them home saying, "Sorry. Plans have changed. I need to put a hold on this whole orphanage plan until I get Adama home." I had to follow through with the orphanage. Too many people's lives were hanging in the balance. Too many orphaned children were desperate for the safety zone we were trying to create. But the thing about Sierra Leone is that *everything* is up for negotiation. I looked the Minister of Social Welfare dead in the eye and said, "Will you promise me, if I place a hold on my case, you will let me process through next month, if I come back?" He looked at me and, with certainty, said yes. He promised me I could come back if I waited at least 30 days and that he would approve my case for court. She was my child. He knew that and would fight for that. I can't believe I actually believed him.

My stomach was so nervous I skipped coffee that morning. I could hear the honking of the car outside and quickly made my way down the steps and out the door. I won't lie, for the first time in a long time there was a slight skip in my step. Somehow, I felt hopeful. A feeling that had become foreign and distant until now.

Today was gonna be a good day. At least that's what I kept telling myself. Today I had a plan. Today we would make progress.

We made our way through town. The traffic was awful as usual, and, my God, it was freaking hot. I was pouring sweat. As I reached for my water bottle, I realized I had forgotten it. I suppose in planning for my visit with Adama I forgot to pack my own things. Oh well. I didn't need it. I could make it through the day without it. Surely this meeting wouldn't take long. I'd find a road-side stand afterward and stock up before making the long trip to the orphanage where Adama was living.

We turned into the compound where the Ministry of

Social Welfare was located. Unfortunately, this place was like a second home to me. Not the kind you want to go back to; it's the kind you hope you can forget. I had the compound memorized. The way the buildings would lean, as if worn out by what went on inside them, groaning and aching just like me. There were always so many people just standing around as if they had nothing better to do than to sit by watching worlds come undone around them. Sadly, the ministry wasn't very good at things like adoption or family reunification. Back then they were not very good at advocating for justice, nor speaking up for children and women who could not speak for themselves. So, there was little to rejoice about around there. It was mostly drama, conversations that never resulted in action, and loads of pain.

The cutting kind.

We pulled right up to the entrance and parked the car, as we had done hundreds of times before. Of course, we caused heads to turn. White people showing up to the ministry only meant controversy. The people lingering about would be sure to stick around to find out what was happening and the reason behind our visit. I usually found myself cursing under my breath when we would get comments and stares, annoyed at the abusive behavior and ignorance. After a while, being called a child trafficker gets a little old. But today the crowd didn't bother me. Today I was going to win. Today I would see my child again.

I quickly tried to wrap my mind around the agenda as I walked in. We had a lot to accomplish, and we needed the ministry's support in a variety of areas. At the end of our meeting, my plan was to request permission to visit Adama, just as I had done so many, many times before. I had also gathered up the courage to ask for her to be moved to our center again. We had been denied in the past, but I felt like this time it could be different.

Maybe this day would be our lucky one. Today they would say yes.

We waited on the woman hosting the meeting. She was always very slow to welcome us in, putting our meeting at the bottom of her list of priorities. We would sometimes sit for hours on end, in the sweltering heat. Hours would pass, and my patience would wear thin. But this wasn't my country. I knew that full well. So, patience became a virtue I tried to hold onto, even though I wanted to murder someone on most days.

We were finally ushered into a tiny office. It felt overwhelmingly dark and stale. I remember the smell that day — a combination of Cassava leaves and fish. It was just after lunch, and the smell was nauseating to me.

When we were wrapping up, I took the chance to request my visit to Adama's orphanage. I also spit out my hope to have her moved. It tumbled out of my mouth so fast, before I could let my nerves talk me out of it. I'm sure I was over-emotional and that my tears were brimming. I had trouble controlling myself in those settings. I cared so deeply about our work there and the government never did. They never cared. I hated showing my feelings in front of them. When my defenses were shattered it was as though they would armor up. I could feel their smirks invade the room. They knew my passion meant a payday for them.

What happened next was debilitating.

The woman across the desk — who I refuse to name because she still holds power in the city and would close our orphanage down if given the chance — leaned in.

She stared at me, strangely, like she was peering right through me. Her mind was on something else entirely. I felt like maybe I should say it all again in case she didn't hear me. The awkward silence somehow felt dangerous to me. As soon as I opened my mouth and began to repeat myself, she interrupted me.

Adama? You are asking me to see Adama. The small pikin? Why? Do you not know? Has no one told you?

I quickly turned toward Osseh, my closest Sierra Leonian confidant, and scanned his face, hoping he had some idea of where this conversation was going. And if he did know, why was I in the dark? I tried to read his expression. He looked just as confused as I did. He leaned in, adjusting his chair and focusing in on the woman behind the desk. He said, "No. We are not aware of anything regarding Adama. What are you trying to say Mrs. _____?"

I felt a cry rise in my throat. I still didn't know why. I felt numb and as though I were on the edge of a cliff. The unknown was below me, and I was being forced to jump into it. This conversation was taking me to a dark place, a place I didn't want to be dragged into. I wasn't ready. Yet I could feel there was no choice. I knew what was coming next would break me. I could feel it in my bones, an eerie, sick, disgusting feeling that soon would suffocate the entire room. The room got hotter and hotter. The sweat poured down my face and soaked through my clothes. Even though I could hear the fan spinning in the background, even though I could feel the wind off the blades blowing against my back, there was no air in the room. I was on fire. I was losing my breath.

The room was so quiet. And then her voice pierced through my thoughts.

Well, I am sorry to say, she is dead.

I stared at her. Everything slowed down. I felt the sting, a burning sensation invading my body. I was unable to speak, unable to process her words. I was unable to do anything at all.

She's dead.

Osseh's voice broke through and took center stage.

How? When? What happened? No one called me. Someone should have called me.

I could tell he was as angry as I was. He had been her guardian angel. He had watched over her and checked in every single month while I was in the States, sending me photographs and loving her for me. He was her Uncle Osseh. I knew this was killing him on the inside, too.

I interrupted Osseh, reaching over and placing my hand on his leg, as if to slow him down.

Wait. Are you sure? Are you sure it was my Adama? Can you check? Can you make sure? Please. There must be a mistake. I know there has to be confusion here. She is fairly healthy. I've been sending support. There is no way it's my Adama.

The woman continued shuffling paperwork, trying to find our file and mumbling under her breath. She began telling us a story, as though it were fictional, about someone else. But it wasn't about someone else.

It was Adama's story. Her last chapter.

She had gotten a call from the orphanage late in the night. A child had died.

Malaria. At least that's what they said.

Supposedly they were treating her, but according to

the report she quickly developed a fever. The fever was rapid and progressed so fast that they were unable to help her. At least that's what they said.

She began convulsing. They loaded her into a vehicle and drove her to the nearest hospital on the east side of town. But on the way her brain hemorrhaged. By the time they got there it was too late.

All of this, according to the report. The report she was having trouble finding.

I asked her to repeat everything she said, everything they had said. Over and over again.

Then I told her to call Ina at the orphanage. As much arguing and fighting as we had done over this child in the past, I was sure she had the number saved and on speed dial.

Ma'am. I believe you have the wrong child. I would have been called. Osseh would have been called. I need you to call them NOW. RIGHT NOW.

My voice was getting louder. I was trying to remain stable and in control. I could feel Osseh leaning in, wanting to remind me with his presence to stay calm but also knowing there was no way I could stay calm.

She picked up her cell phone and dialed the number. I could hear the ringing from where I sat. I heard a voice answer. The woman behind the desk began speaking in Krio. I could hear the person on the other end speaking loudly and furiously. It was like a tennis match. The woman was nodding her head, and I felt Osseh's presence shift. Then he put his head into his hands. I knew at that moment what that meant. He had done it so many times before. When things were spiraling, when a situation would move from bad to worse. I would watch him place his head in his hands, sigh a deep sigh, and pray. I could see now this was one of those times. As he began to pray, I began losing faith in the God he was praying to, realizing this was a moment my faith may not ever recover from.

I lost my breath.

She hung up the phone. And in a matter of fact tone stated,

Yes, I was correct. The child was Adama. She is dead. I am sorry you were not notified. She has already been buried.

Osseh stepped in again. I don't remember what he said or what the woman said after that. All I could think about were my daughter's eyes and her heartbeat against my chest. The giggle that would explode from her little body when I would kiss her neck. All I could think about was our last visit. How I never held her. How I stared at her from across the room, willing her to look my direction. And when she did, the way it felt, as if we were the only two in the room. Did she wonder why I didn't go to her? Did she feel the sting? The sting I felt?

I'd chosen the opening of an orphanage over her. I refused to give a bribe. I trusted the government to protect her. And they failed.

I failed. I failed my daughter. She was dead because of me.

I stood up slowly, anger rising. I'm not sure who or what my anger was directed at. Was I angry at the government? Was I angry at this woman who delivered the news? Or was I angry at myself? I still don't know. But the anger was there, and it was fierce.

I began to shift blame.

This is your fault! Adama had a way out! I was her mother. She had a home! There was an answer for her. YOU chose not to act on her behalf. YOU kept her in that place. She is dead because of YOU. And I will never be able to forgive you for doing this. For keeping us apart. For making me choose. You promised me she would come home. All the time we wasted. THIS is on you.

I said all of that in my mind, screaming at the top of my lungs. But I realized in that moment that we were all the enemy.

I got up, walked toward the door, and turned only to say one thing.

This was OUR fault.

She said nothing. Her face was stone cold. She continued shuffling papers, nodding her head, refusing to make eye contact with me. I knew she was done. Soon I would be ushered from her office.

My tears were brimming, and I wanted to keep them for myself. She didn't deserve to know how much pain I was in. I wouldn't let them spill out with her in the room. I gathered my bag and smoothed my dress, trying desperately to hold it together. I told Osseh it was time to go.

We made our way to the car. Now the tears were streaming. My heart was exploding. It took everything in me not scream and moan and fall out right in the middle of the compound.

But people were watching.

Fucking people were always watching.

I quickly climbed into the car. Placed my sunglasses over my eyes and cried. Counting between breaths.

10.9.8.7.6.5.4.3.2.1.

We pulled out slowly, as in a funeral procession. Only we were not in a funeral procession. Supposedly she had been buried without me. Where? I didn't know, but I would find out.

To be honest I can't remember if I began my quest for truth that day or the next. It's all a haze. And trying to remember, as I write these words, feels like a knife in my chest.

3.

THE HAZE
2011

*See, the darkness is leaking from the crack.
I cannot contain it.*
—Sylvia Plath, *Three Women*

I wish I could walk you through what happened next, moment by moment. But I can't. The memories don't exist. I can't remember the drive back to the guest house. I don't even remember calling home after I found out about Adama's death. I have a vague picture tucked up inside my brain, but it's mostly shadows. I can remember standing outside the guest house compound. I can remember a struggle to get my call to go through. I would dial the number, put the phone up to my ear, it would ring a few times and then go dead. Nothing new. Cell service was a luxury back then. I know that I did call and get through to my family at some point because they all clearly remember the day. Jason tells me he can remember where he was when the phone rang. He happened to be out of town, spending the day with the kids and his parents. They were visiting antique malls and eating blackberry cobbler at The Bellbuckle Cafe. He was having a perfect afternoon nestled in the hills of Tennessee.

Then I called.

I asked Jason what he can recall about that day. He said he remembers feeling helpless, having no control over anything, too many miles between us. I was on the other side of the world. He was trying to keep it together in front of the kids. He contacted our other relatives and friends who needed to be in the know. I often wonder how he handled repeating himself over and over again. Did the words sting every time he said them? Was it a bitter pill for him too? I wonder what the reaction was as he went through the list of family and friends. It's hard to know because so few people have ever had the guts to talk about Adama in my presence since it all happened. It's sad, isn't it? That we all struggle sitting inside the pain. As much as we want to crowd in and support our loved ones in crisis, sometimes we do just the opposite. When comments like, "God just loved her so much he took her home" prove void we just stop sitting inside the wreckage with the person who is imprisoned by it. We leave them. We never ask. We never speak of the grief. It's all just too uncomfortable when the prayers didn't work, when death has the final say.

Jason and I circled around the depth of our loss for years and never discussed it. We still sometimes struggle to talk about it. As I write this, I realize I've never really asked him what it was like for him the day I told him our daughter had died. I've never asked him what he went through. I suppose my pain was heavy enough, and maybe I failed when it came to helping him carry his own. Actually, there is no maybe. I failed my husband. It's a shame how grief comes in, stealing our ability to empathize, to connect, taking our memories captive and simply changing us.

The one flashback I have, the one place that isn't all shadows, is the loneliness. I can remember it very well. The empty space that made itself at home that night, and then decided to stay for good.

It may sound odd to say I still feel alone in my grief after seven years. But I do. I am sure there have been people along the way who have tried to help me, but I have pushed people out of the wreckage. After all, it was mine to sift through, mine to sort out and reckon with. Besides I didn't want anyone to move anything. It's like spending too much time with anyone else in my disaster zone could chance some part of Adama being erased. I didn't want anyone explaining away her death, nor moving the blame from where I knew it should sit. I didn't want anyone using clichés and sympathy statements as balm for my open wounds. I wanted to keep it all close. I wanted to be alone in it. I deserved to be alone. It was all on me. I think it's a space I will never leave. Filling it would seem foreign. The empty space Adama left has become a shrine in my life. The loneliness is a constant dedication to remembering her and to holding myself accountable, somehow making her life mean something. And making her death mean something even more.

That night, I wanted to crawl into my bunk bed at the guest house, switch on the fan so I wouldn't hear the conversations coming from downstairs, and secure the mosquito net. That way the rest of the world, including rodents and anything else that crawled across the floor in the night, couldn't get in. I wanted to lay in the pitch black. I wouldn't have minded if the darkness had taken me that night and kept me for a while. Maybe forever. Settling into the nothingness would mean I wouldn't have to feel a thing. I wouldn't have to face the truth.

The truth. What was the truth?

The guilt rising in my bones told me the truth was something I couldn't handle. I can't explain the physical and emotional state I was in. It was the first time I felt anxiety, the unwelcome intruder that attacks your body in times like this. It gets a grip on you and puts a knife right through your chest. The tightness and pressure weighing on me shut my body down. I stayed in bed barely able to move. There were a few other Americans staying at the guest house, and they would check on me every so often. Their words and facial expressions made me want to scream bloody murder. I know everyone meant well. But the glances at one another while trying to calm me down, the comments about God having some grand plan, were not what I needed to hear. The continued whispers about how this would be used for some bigger purpose, and the pity, was more than I could swallow. I needed everyone to just leave me be. Each time I would hear their steps on the stairs I would beg God to send them away. The God I didn't believe in anymore, the one who never showed up.

I tried to breathe through it. But honestly it felt better to hold my breath. Everything was out of control. The only thing I could control in that moment was the breathing in and the breathing out. Stubbornly I wanted to stop the breathing. If I could have suffocated myself that night I probably would have. The guilt was stronger than the grief. The guilt took over and gained complete control of my mind. It took me to places the grief never could. Places I couldn't come back from. Even still today.

Usually when I struggle, I immerse myself in music. It's always been my safe place, my escape, where I find hope and resolution. You would have thought my headphones would have been the arms that held me that night, that I would be looking for solace of some sort. But I preferred the silence. I needed to think. Solace wasn't what I needed at all. I needed ANSWERS. I needed to DO SOMETHING. Obviously, I couldn't turn back the clock. I couldn't change it. It was done. But I sure as hell wouldn't just go back to the States without getting to the bottom of it all. I realized that day that Adama had been a statistic all along. I may have called her my daughter, but to the rest of the world, she had no name. She was invisible. She was a number, a file that had been misplaced. An orphan without a paper trail. Nothing to define or prove she had ever even existed. That may have represented her life, but it would not represent her in death. It would not be her legacy. She would count. Somehow. I would make sure of it.

The level of desperation I felt to find truth, to figure out what really happened, and to rescue Adama, even in death, was familiar territory for me. Except in all the times before, the loss hadn't come from my own doing. I was always playing superhero, thinking I could save the world from its own game. Until now, I had done a fairly good job at exposing injustice and making a dent in the orphan crisis.

But now what? I could no longer pretend I was the good guy. I could no longer sound the alarm on injustice when I was part of the problem. In exposing it, I would expose myself.

I was okay with that. It was time to take my lessons from the before. I had to find the spark in my bones. Pain would be the kindle. I would light myself on fire in an attempt to fix this. My mind took me back to the beginning, to what started it all, the reason I was across the world mourning my daughter in the first place.

4.

BEFORE THE DAY THAT CHANGED EVERYTHING
2001

You may choose to look the other way but you can never say again that you did not know. —William Wilberforce, Speech before the House of Commons, 1791

My first adopted daughter came into my life like a freight train. My day began much like the day Adama was taken from me. It was every bit normal. Nothing out of the ordinary. No sign telling me my world was about to shift on its axis.

It was 2001. I was 23 years old. I was a stay at home mom at the time, living in a small town in Missouri. Jason worked for the church as a full-time youth pastor. I stayed at home and spent my days raising our son and offering support to Jason and the church wherever I could. Everyday was the same. Get up, feed the baby, do the laundry, clean up the house. Repeat. I loved my life, but it wasn't easy. Jason was gone a lot, immersed in being everything the church had expected him to be. He always did so well handling the expectations of the people. But it wasn't as easy for me. I never quite fit the mold. I never seemed to be able to measure up. Trying to be what everyone wanted me to be wore me down to almost nothing. I spent a lot of time alone. I loved my husband, and I loved my son. But I was young and I felt like something was missing. I felt small and insignificant. Invisible in a sense. It wasn't that I wanted to be seen; I just needed to do something that mattered, something that made me feel as though the space I was taking up in the world was intentional. I felt like there had to be more to life than the one I had created. I felt pulled. I was unsettled in my heart and was searching for something. I just didn't know what.

I thought that by being a youth pastor's wife I had a pretty good handle on suffering. My job was to counsel and be of service to youth in our local church. Leading teens is no easy task, but it was the only area of our ministry that I really did connect with. I loved the kids. I adored them actually. I loved the chaos, the mess, and the hearts we fought for. I loved what restoration looked like, and I was always hopeful the children would become world changers if we could just give them the tools they needed. Maybe they would go into the world I had never been able to see with my own eyes. Maybe they would be the generation that would change things.

We also did our small part to aid in the suffering of others around the world by holding annual fundraisers. God, I make it sound like we deserved a medal or something. It makes me sick even typing those words. We never got our hands dirty when it came to international giving and support. No one traveled. God forbid we actually leave the comfort of that little town and actually face the rest of the world and embrace humanity. It was always simply about money. Why would we sit with the poor, when we could just send money and call it a day? We would send the check off to our church headquarters, knowing someone, somewhere, would benefit. That's as deep into the waters of international mission work that I had ever been. I knew nothing else. We raised money, gave pats on the back to all who contributed, and considered that enough. I was good with that. I had to be good with that. The blinders I was wearing, the ones I wore because everyone else wore the same kind, kept me from realizing that the ignorance I lived in daily was anything but something I should be "good" with.

I had been taught that my life could be used for a greater good — but with conditions. I truly believe this mindset set me on a path of choosing to love conditionally, to give conditionally, and to serve conditionally. Not exactly a period of my life I am proud of.

I realize now that the past can shape us. Circumstance can dictate the direction we travel, but, in the end, our purpose always seems to find a way to turn the tide, to shift the sand. At some point when we least expect it, we receive an invitation to embrace humanity.

At some point we always collide with our calling. Our calling is discovered in the YES. The moment we say yes to where we have been invited, and we settle in for the ride. That's when the collision occurs. It's that collision that ignites a fire, creating an explosion on the inside. It's that explosion that burns up everything we have ever known. We are left with ashes. And from those ashes we eventually rise, but we will rise different.

The day my life changed, the day I was stripped of all apathy, the day my blinders were lifted came at me like a tsunami. Waves of injustice and rushing waters of grief knocked me over, taking with it everything I ever thought I knew. It left me stunned and in shock.

Seventeen years later, the shock has yet to subside.

I had just laid my son Jordan down for a nap. I walked into the kitchen and picked up a newspaper. Inside was an advertisement for a Steven Curtis Chapman concert. I was a big fan at the time and couldn't wait to see him in concert. As I read through the article I found myself reading the story of his recent international adoption from China. A little girl.

International adoption? What is that? I had never heard of such a thing —ironic seeing where my life is today — how pathetic. I was intrigued and kept reading. Before I knew it, I was getting a crash course on the latest orphan statistics around the world. I sat stunned for a moment, not sure what to make of what I had just read. I couldn't wrap my brain around *why* I didn't know about this. I parked myself in front of my computer and the rest of the day was a blur. I found myself drowning in photos, thousands of them online, picturing children all over the world living in orphanages, alone and without a family.

How did I not know about this? How was I not aware? What I was seeing was an international crisis, and I was totally clueless. Talk about injustice. I was raised in church my entire life, always made it to Sunday school, sang in the choir, raised money for missionaries, taught classes at the nursing home, attended discipleship class. I had quite the resume. HOW DID I NOT KNOW? Why had no one ever told me? I was searching for an excuse to make myself feel less guilt and to this day I still don't have one. It makes me sick.

So began my plight to learn all I could about the crisis that haunted me in my sleep. I studied Haiti, China, India, and the United States. I settled in on countries like Guatemala, Thailand, and Russia. Stories of abandonment, abuse, neglect and trafficking kept me up at night. A sense of responsibility swept over me and pushed me into action. I wasn't sure what that "action" needed to look like, but I knew I could never continue on as if I didn't know.

It's interesting how different the journey had been for me and for Jason. Once the shades of ignorance were removed from our eyes, I couldn't stop staring. I couldn't escape the images and the computer became a permanent attachment to my body. It was like I wanted to be tortured, almost as though I enjoyed it. I welcomed the invitation. I would sit for hours staring into the eyes of children, envisioning their stories, knowing their pasts would shake me to my core if I really knew the trauma they had experienced. I couldn't get enough. I joined chat rooms about adoption and orphans. I signed up for online newsletters showcasing work being done to raise awareness around the world, and I began to get angry. Angry that my little town in the boot heel of Missouri was perfectly comfortable not knowing anything about what I had discovered, and equally disturbed that my husband also couldn't bear to look into the eyes of the children I had dug out of an online grave.

I'm not sure what his heart and head was telling him in those days. Maybe he was scared of what he didn't know. Disturbed too, by the fact that no one had ever exposed him to the suffering in the world and afraid of why that may have been the case. He was realizing that the church may not have been all we thought it was, and maybe he was embarrassed to admit that ignoring human suffering made our hearts ugly. When you begin to recognize that ugliness, you have no choice but to shift and somehow change your mindset. For Jason, that also meant changing a culture within the walls of our church and even our own family. He knew it may mean leaving the church altogether, and I'm not sure he was ready for that. He wanted things to stay the same. It was easier that way. It was easier to just keep pretending we didn't know.

I can still feel the catch in my breath. That moment when the clock stopped, and I was introduced to my first daughter. I was still in front of that computer, as I had been for several months. Aimlessly, clicking through ID numbers. Was I shopping for a child? I don't know. Some may call it that. I do know Jason and I had yet to speak about adoption. I can honestly say I'm not sure what I was looking for. I do know I was searching. I was searching for a place to start, searching for a heart to hold, seeking out a way to somehow make right what was so terribly wrong.

Then I saw her. She was tagged incorrectly.

Her ID read:

63669-Boy-Africa-DOB-Aug171999.

I was spending most of my time searching through stories of little boys. In the back of my mind thinking that if we adopt someday maybe we could adopt a little boy so Jordan would have a brother. That would be perfect. They would fit into our family so nicely.

Wow. I was so naïve. There I was creating a box for my sweet little adopted child to live inside. I had no idea what I was getting into and no idea how much I had to learn, how much my heart and mind would need to be stretched to become even half of what an orphan child would need me to be. I kept thinking I would "save" him, not knowing it would be the children who would save me.

I clicked on the ID number that I thought would fit so nicely into our perfect little family and found myself staring into the eyes of a little itty-bitty girl. Her eyes sparkled, and her smile wrecked me. She shattered my plans and screamed at me from my computer in a voice I will never forget.

Do you see me? I NEED YOU TO SEE ME.

I heard her voice through the windows of her soul. Her eyes continued to beckon me, and I couldn't turn away. Her photograph was everything. *Everything* to me from that moment on.

The next few days were really a blur. I couldn't focus on anything at all except locating this mystery child. I felt it a disgrace that she was listed with an ID number and not a name, saddened that her photo was nestled in among thousands of others just waiting to be noticed, chosen, and remembered. I did the only thing I knew to do at the time. I set out to locate this child and prepared my speech of the century. I thought the toughest obstacle I had ahead of me was convincing Jason this child was our daughter. I wish I had been right.

Jason was a trooper. Yes, at first, I think he thought I had lost my mind. We talked about this child for days, and then the days turned to months. The time that passed seemed like an eternity and the burden I carried seemed to become heavier and heavier with each passing day. What if he and I never landed on the same page? What would that mean? I knew this child was my daughter. So if that was the case, why hadn't God told Jason the same thing? What did this mean for our marriage?

Through those conversations we experienced tears, anger, frustration, and grief. I cried tears because I felt so strongly we needed to find this little girl and rescue her. Not because we had the ability to save but because I felt I had been rescued myself. I felt an urgency I could not escape, and I couldn't let her go. I felt anger, because Jason didn't see the travesty I saw. For him the greater frustration was knowing that we would likely get little support from family and friends. He felt certain our church would never support it. At that time in our life we were overly concerned about the opinions of others. Their opinions ruled our lives.

The darkest days of our marriage rose up during the early days of our adoption. I look back and can see now that the odds were most definitely against us.

Our lives were about to shift and we would not be silent about what we saw. It was just the beginning. We were beginning to wage war, a battle we would never back down from. It was time to begin, and the universe, the power against us, whatever you want to call it, was conspiring to stop what was about to happen.

In the end, by making the decision to fight for Jayda, we faced the kind of grief you feel when your plans have been dashed, knowing you are about to embark on a journey that will most definitely change your life. It was intense, but in the end we embraced the uncertainties for her. After all, she was worth it. Her life meant more than the comfort of everyday life, the comfort of being able to turn a blind eye. Her life meant more than all the relationships we might lose in our quest to find her. So began the journey that led us down lonely, broken roads and into silent caves of more apathy and injustice.

5.

WAITING GAMES
2001

*I am weary with my crying out; my throat is parched.
My eyes grow dim with waiting for my God.*
—Psalm 69:3

Making the decision to adopt Jayda changed everything. Our world was already different, and she hadn't even come home yet. Looking back now, it's obvious that when we stepped off the cliff of adoption, Jason was wearing shades of reality. I, on the other hand, was wearing shades of idealism and lived in the land of pure bliss. I just assumed that everyone would be as excited as I was, that everyone would take one look at her photograph and just know she was meant to be ours. I was sure they would see those beautiful eyes and know she was worth the fight, worth it all.

It didn't happen like that.

It's so hard to talk about this period in our life because I know Jayda will eventually read this chapter, and she will know the truth. She will know that, for many, she wasn't worth the cost, the strain, the grueling process. She wasn't worth the second glances or worth becoming an interracial family. She will know that there are people who love her very much now, but back then they would have nothing to do with bringing her home. I am at peace with this now. Adopting Jayda wouldn't be the first time we felt isolated. It would only prepare us for what was coming, for the person I was becoming. I know that now.

So where was this child?

Good question. All we had was a photo online. I contacted the webmaster to find out who had contributed the photograph to the site and got a name of an adoption facilitator out of California. I reached out to the facilitator and talked to a really sweet lady who shared with me everything she knew about this little girl who had captured my heart.

She was two years old. According to the woman, she had been born in a refugee camp, abandoned to the center by her mother, and had no siblings. (I would find out many years later that some of her story was bogus, but we will get to that eventually). She shared with me that she was living in an orphanage in Sierra Leone, West Africa.

Sierra Leone?

Where was that? I grabbed the globe in my son's room and finally located the country. I had never heard of it before. The next several days I combed the internet trying to find out everything I could about this tiny little country that was just a speck on the globe, the size of South Carolina. Everything I found online was shocking and excruciating to read. A decade-long civil war had just ended. The photos online literally made me weep. How could I have not known about this? People were being traded, exploited, maimed, and murdered at the hands of rebels all over the diamond trade. Thousands were displaced. Thousands more were now amputees. Children were orphaned, and I had no idea. It made me sick inside. How had this not made national news? Maybe it had, but it clearly hadn't been aired in my area of the country.

I couldn't sleep. I would dream about this little girl, and I would envision what it must have been like for her and her family. How could a two-year-old be uprooted by rebels, lose everything, end up in a refugee camp, abandoned by her mother, and still manage to smile for a camera?

I knew it might take me years to get my mind wrapped around her loss, to restore her spirit, but I knew I would spend the rest of my life trying.

We knew we had to act quickly. I had read that one in every three children were dying before the age of five in Sierra Leone. In my mind the quicker we moved the faster she would get home and be safe.

The fundraising alone almost killed us. It was a weary road since we had so few supporting our plans. First up was a home study. From a legal perspective, the home study had to be done. The state department needs assurances that your home is safe and that you are capable of raising an adopted child. Immigration paperwork was also a necessity that came with a hefty price tag. We had decided to try to pay for all the paperwork on our own. Then once we were officially matched and approved by the government, we would begin raising support. This was no easy task. Jason worked as a youth pastor for a rather small church and made about $10 an hour. We barely had a penny to our name. I stayed at home at the time since Jordan was so small but quickly realized that in order to make this adoption happen I would have to find work outside the home. So I did.

I began working at the local newspaper office in the advertising department. We used everything we could save to cover the first expenses to get our adoption process going.

Once we were officially matched and approved, we began the grueling task of raising the adoption fees. It seemed almost impossible. We sent letters to family and friends. A few responded with so much support

I would sit and just cry over their kind words. It was like a flowing spring in dry and hostile desert. It seemed that every time we mere met with opposition, God would send someone else our way who understood our quest and stood with us — even if it wasn't who we had hoped it would be.

Our letters to family and friends yielded support but not near enough. We had to make a decision to either back out or pray for a miracle. Backing out was never an option. So we did what every adoptive family does. We worked extra jobs. We sold donuts (800 dozen!). We emptied furniture out of our home and sold it all on Craigslist. And we prayed for a miracle. Within a few weeks we had raised what was necessary to begin the adoption process. We sent a big fat check, and then the waiting began.

I wish I could tell you that during the waiting I created a memory book filled with the fairytale moments, documenting our journey to bring Jayda home. I can't. I wish I could say that adoption was as lovely and beautiful as feeling a baby move inside your womb for the first time or that the reactions from family and friends were as picture perfect as the reactions that come with the news of a natural pregnancy. I guess at the time we were so burdened with the shoes we were walking in we never even thought about taking the time to recall the steps we had taken. At the time, I doubt we had any interest in remembering most of it. Still, there were moments I do remember, moments that were mind numbing and others that took my breath away in a good way.

The wait was so painful, and there were only a handful of people we could share the intimate details of our journey with. Most of our family and friends rarely asked how things were going. It was the giant elephant in the room. I'm not sure what hurt worse — never being asked, as though Jayda didn't exist, or being asked, responding, and then dealing with the common response.

Well if it's God's will, it will all work out.

Bullshit. That's what I really wanted to say.

I wanted to scream at the top of my lungs every single time I was met by one particularly loud and opinionated woman in the halls of the church. She managed to corner me every month or so. She would pull her glasses down her nose so she could peek out above them, and, with almost a sneer, she would say,

I've been praying for you and Jason, honey, that God would just speak to you and make it clear to you the path he wants you to take. He only helps those who help themselves, and those people over there... well they have a lot of work to do before God helps them out, ya know.

She did know, didn't she, that "God helps those who help themselves" was *scripture,* written by some pulpit preacher, and not part of the *Bible* at all?

Then there was the time she caught me on the stairs and asked me to see a recent picture of Jayda. When I obliged and handed her one from my purse, she said,

Hmmm. What a pretty little girl, but I'm not so sure God planned for families to look so different from one another. We need to pray she finds a family that will look more like her. That would be so much easier on her and especially on you.

Seriously I wanted to claw her eyes out.

The last straw came on a Sunday evening. We had a few awesome church members who really did care about us, and our child living across the world, and they wanted to help us. They held a spaghetti dinner to raise money for us. We were given the opportunity to share about our journey and why we felt called to adopt. We raised a few hundred dollars and were ecstatic. We had several church members come up to us and apologize for not seeing the full picture and promised to pray for us and that the adoption would be finalized soon. On our way out, a female church member approached me. She took me to the corner and told me that God had spoken to her during our dinner. She said God told her that the reason we are facing such a long wait and so much opposition is because it's not God's will to put black babies in white families. She said Jayda would be better off staying in the refugee camp where people who were the same color could take care of her.

I almost lost my religion that night.

I went into quite the tailspin. It was evident to us

that our child would face great scrutiny and would not be accepted by the majority in our church, and I just wasn't good with that. I was tired of trying to convince everyone that adopting a child who was orphaned, a child who would likely die without intervention, was actually a good idea. I could not wrap my brain around how the church was filled with members who claimed they loved Jesus, claimed they were there to be a part of the greater good, to serve and love the least of these, yet lived with such condition and hate in their hearts. The contempt they held for anyone who didn't look like them or believe like them made me physically sick. I could no longer deal with it. I was tired of being surrounded by calloused individuals. I could no longer pretend that everything would be okay. I knew that we had to leave our small town, not only for Jayda, but for our own sanity.

We moved multiple times during our wait and eventually left the boot heel of Missouri and headed for a more culturally diverse life in Nashville. It was the right choice. I had a passion for music and wanted to pursue a career in the music business. The church wasn't where I felt my purpose sat, and Jason knew that. Thankfully he supported my heart for music and was my biggest supporter. He found a church in Nashville he could relocate to. I set my sights on a dream, and preparing for our little girl to come home, away from all the judgment. We settled smack dab in the middle of Music City.

We continued to wear the season of waiting like a

heavy coat in the middle of a stifling summer. We felt such a burden and such a weight and yet we were stuck.

We waited over three years for our first court order. I say "first" because we eventually received news that voided the order altogether. Those three years were likely filled with the same dark days others who have walked the adoption road experienced. We had the decorated room with clothes hung neatly in a closet. As each year passed we would pack up the clothes she had outgrown and buy new ones. We had books on a shelf and stuffed animals sitting on a bed. We would learn to keep the door closed because what was inside the room only made the gaping hole that Jayda's absence created that much deeper. I do remember that the longer we waited and the more time that passed, most people in our lives truly believed the adoption would never happen. I actually had a family member call our Jayda a "lost cause" and "not meant to be." Talk about a knife to the heart. While the outside world looking in viewed our wait as silly and something we should move on from, the wait for us only bred a deeper passion for this child we had never met.

One memory I held close during that standstill was a cold Thursday morning. I was headed to the office and in the passenger seat next to me sat a stack of unopened mail. While sitting at a never-ending red light I grabbed the stack and quickly started sifting through. I came across an envelope from the orphanage that was caring for our daughter. It was very strange and out of the norm to get something from them in the mail. I think we may have only received six photos of her during the entire wait. Quickly tearing it open I pulled out a single piece of white construction paper. On it were tiny little circles, drawn in all colors, filling the page. Carefully written, in the top right hand corner, I found my daughter's name. As tears streamed down my face I began crying and screaming at the top of my lungs. I was finally holding something my daughter had also held in her hands. It was the closest I had ever come to actually feeling her next to me. I traced the curves of every circle, kissed that piece of paper over and over again, and carried it with me for 19 more months.

My office space at work was filled with photos of Jayda. Every time the agency would send me a new photo, I would proudly parade it around the office. The girls I had made friends with were all so supportive, and it was a breath of fresh air from what we had known before. I also had a friend who walked the entire journey with me. Kelly. She was someone who understood taking a stand for what she believed in. She had also lost several relationships chasing dreams others couldn't understand. She and I became very close through that season. She was my rock though the hard years. I am sure my emotional roller coaster weighed her down, but she never complained. In fact, her office was just down the hall from mine, and her space was decorated with Jayda's photos too. She was a proud honorary aunt, and it meant the world to me to have her on our side.

I can remember one particular day so well. Kelly and I were walking into the office from the parking lot, and I just lost it. I completely broke down. It wasn't the first time and it wouldn't be the last time. I told her that day that I wasn't sure how much longer I could take the waiting. I told her I felt like God had left the building. It felt as though he had just disappeared in the middle of it all. His silence was deafening and that bred such a sense of isolation. I told her maybe he wasn't real after all. How could he just leave me like this? I told her that it seemed like bringing Jayda home was impossible and I felt the pressure to let go. She looked at me and said,

You can't let go. I won't let you.

And she didn't.

6.

THE PLAN
2011

Her absence is like the sky, spread over everything.
—CS Lewis, *A Grief Observed*

I am sure I called Kelly and told her about Adama at some point. Or maybe Jason called her. I can't really recall. How I ached to have my best friend with me. She had walked me through the ups and downs of Jayda's adoption, the opening of the orphanage — a story I haven't even started to tell you yet. She knew losing Adama after everything we had been through to bring her home would be something I might not ever recover from. I had wanted to call her that morning, to run my plan by her. But it was six hours ahead in Freetown. It was the middle of the night where she was. I decided against waking her and mapped out the plan on my own.

Every so often the pain and the reality would bombard me, leaving me in pieces, wrecked and weeping. The pouring out felt guttural, primal. I was still trying to wrap my brain and heart around Adama being gone. I had more tears than the ocean could hold. So, I just kept letting them out.

Through the night I asked questions and drew conclusions. Oh, the stories I was telling myself. The nightmare I was living. "If only" continued on a loop, chasing every other thought out of my mind. It's interesting how guilt grips us. Even so, by morning I had created a plan that was in full swing.

1. *Find out what really happened to Adama.*

I didn't buy that malaria killed her. It may have contributed, but, give me a break. Did they think we were that stupid? It made no sense. At the time the country was offering free medical care for children under five. It was very rare to die from malaria anymore. The meds were almost always successful in treating the sickness. It hadn't always been this way, but they had made progress. Something just did not make sense. What else happened? Part of the story was missing. I was adamant about getting to the bottom of it. I knew the kind of abuse that followed the children around in that orphanage. Those little ones walked the halls hollowed out like an empty shell, as though they were ghosts who were still living, trying not to feel the pain from the reprimands, the sting of hunger, the shame of sexual abuse. How did I know this? I'd seen it all before. I can remember the first time I stepped foot inside that place. The children didn't come running like in other centers around the city. They peered out from behind barred windows. They hid behind corners of the building and slowly emerged, as though they were trying to decide if we were safe or a threat. Once they felt safe they would grab your hand as though they were holding on for dear life. Their eyes told us everything — as did the bones protruding from their skin. The kids were starving, broken, and abused. What I knew was this: They did something to Adama. Malaria could not have been the only thing responsible for her death. There was more to the story.

2. *Get a copy of her death certificate.*

I was assuming the hospital filed these. I also assumed the doctor's name would be on it, and this is how I would find him. I knew Ina wouldn't give me his name. Just as she held Adama for ransom when she was alive, she would try to keep her from me in death. I had to find a way around her. I was done playing by her rules.

3. *Talk to the doctor who worked her case.*

How long had he been treating Adama? Did she have any other medical conditions that played a part in her system shutting down? How does a brain hemorrhage if a child is receiving proper care? What would make a fever spike that high — especially if she was taking meds? Or was she *not* being treated after all? What was her condition upon arrival? Were there signs she had been neglected? I already knew the answer to that. Of course she had been neglected; neglect is what almost took her life years before. How long did she live once she made it to the hospital? I needed to know everything. EVERYTHING. I would pay him off. Whatever it took. Whatever he wanted. I had nothing to lose anymore. She was already dead.

4. *Find out where she was buried.*

I was made aware that children were not usually given marked graves. Actually, no one in Sierra Leone was given a grave unless you could afford to spend money on stone. Most people could not, so graves remain unmarked for the majority of those buried. That meant at any moment Adama could be dug up and someone else would be buried in her place, her remains tossed in the trash. I couldn't wrap my brain around this kind of barbaric and disrespectful behavior. *Not my daughter.* My daughter would be properly buried. My daughter would be honored. But first, I had to find out where they put her body.

5. *Prepare the burial.*

I needed to find someone who could carve the stone. I needed someone who could pour concrete. I needed someone who could stand watch. I knew a white woman burying someone would cause a stir. But I didn't care anymore. It was too late to be concerned with perception. I should have never cared in the first place.

God, why did I give a damn in the first place?

It was morning now. Osseh was honking the horn, anxious to put our plan in motion. I packed nothing but my notebook and tissues. I left the cheerios in my bag as well. I couldn't bear to take them out. That bag hasn't been used since that trip. And the cheerios are still inside.

We decided to head to the death certificate office first. I was sure they would have the death reported somewhere. The doctor would have turned it in, right? I was ready to track down this doctor. He was my golden ticket. He would have the answers I was looking for. He had to have them. The thought of never knowing was a brutal possibility I couldn't face down. At least not yet.

Getting around that morning felt demanding and intrusive. On one hand I wanted to stay in my bunk and function in the lonely space of it all. I was good at hiding when I was broken. I desperately wanted to hide away. On the other hand, I knew I had to mobilize. But I felt pushed. Forced into action for a cause I didn't see coming. I didn't ask for this detour. This wasn't the plan. I felt thrown into a storyline that wasn't mine. Almost like an out-of-body experience. I hated every second.

As I got into the vehicle, I felt a cry begin to swell in my throat. Seeing Osseh again made me physically hurt. His eyes looked so tired. Had he been up all night like me? Was he as tired as I was? Was he as tired of this fight as I was? Was it time to end it and go back to a normal life where we hide away from the ugly in the world? Should we part ways so he can go back to a simple existence, and I can go wrestle with the reality of my loss? Had we made any headway in this Godforsaken country? Or had we spun our wheels and wasted time that ultimately cost lives? These were the thoughts and the questions spinning in my mind.

The traffic was horrible. We were in the car for quite some time. I had no energy for conversation. There was enough going on in my own brain. I couldn't possibly unpack it with anyone else. I opened my notebook and picked up where I left off in the night. I knew there would come a moment — probably today — when I would face the grave where Adama was buried. I knew we would also set up a proper burial. I wanted to make sure I had a letter written to her, ready to be placed in the concrete where it would stay. Words that would cover her like a blanket underneath the soil as her body sunk down deep into the Earth. I also needed words for the tombstone. Something that let the world know what beauty lied beneath the surface. God she was so beautiful. And not just beautiful, she was darling. She was inquisitive and brave. She was feisty and full of spunk and determination. She may have only been three years old, but there was purpose in her bones.

My mind continued to wander, and I thought about my family back home. Wondering if the kids even knew yet. Had Jason told them? How did they respond? Had he visited her bedroom since he got the news? I thought about her clothes hanging neatly in the closet. The grey and white striped sheets that had been on her bed for months, the pale pink comforter, and the velvet stuffed elephant that lay next to her pillow. In the waiting, I would sometimes go sit in her room and hold the elephant and pretend she was there with me, asleep in her crib. I would sit in the rocking chair, sing under my breath, and pray. I wondered, as we made our way through town that morning: All those prayers — did they fall on deaf ears after all? Had God abandoned me in the trench work he called me to do? Did he even call me at all? Was this all my doing? None of it made any sense. As I thought about God's "plan" and his lack of intervention, I got angry and realized I needed to get control of my mind. I was beginning to spiral and that was never good. Losing your control in Sierra Leone was a death sentence when it came to trying to get something accomplished. I had slowly learned the art of staying cool and collected. So, I focused back in, closed my eyes, and finished the letter I had started in the middle of the night, to the daughter I would never see again.

My dear Adama,
I am at a loss on where to begin. I feel that I need to write this letter so that it covers you till we are one day reunited. You lost your life at the age of three. Three years old. It feels strange to say those words, even stranger to share with you such adult feelings, but I'm sure now that you are with your creator you have been given wisdom much greater than even my own mind can comprehend.

I want you to know that I will live the rest of my life wishing there was some way I could make right the injustice you faced in your three short years. I wish I could tell you how sorry I am that I wasn't strong enough to fix it, to rescue you, to somehow change the outcome. I have a part of me deep inside that questions God and why he would allow this to happen. I am sure you know these answers. Oh how I wish I did too.

I can still remember the day I met you, how fragile and yet how beautiful you were. I went home from my visit with you permanently etched in my heart. You filled my dreams every night, my thoughts throughout the day. I knew you were mine yet I was so scared to try, so afraid I might not succeed in rescuing you. But your Uncle Osseh helped us in our cause and we began the road to bring you home. I can still remember your brothers' and sisters' reaction when we told them the news. When they found out they had a baby sister across the world, they were so happy. You brought so much joy to our lives during that time. While I worked on paperwork, daddy began working even harder so we could buy all the special things you would need once you came home. We had a tricycle in the garage, a beautiful bedroom just for you. Grandma helped pick out your furniture and we filled your closet with clothes and toys and books. We were ready, ready to bring you home and keep you with us forever.

In the middle of all the preparations, your life and story moved me into action. The conditions you had been forced to endure moved us to open a children's center so we could make sure other children would never have to face what you had to face. On that trip I truly expected to bring you home. Your bag was packed. Grandma was there, and we were ready for court. But on that trip, in September of 2009, your world and my world forever changed. Evil prevailed, and I lost you.

The pain I felt over having to leave you in that dark place scarred my soul and left me with a broken heart. I tucked you away deep down inside and kept you there, never speaking of it, never giving my pain wings through words, only praying that God would protect you till the day he brought you back to me. I didn't realize at the time that the answer to that prayer would mean you would lose your life. For you, the only rescue was to take you to meet Jesus. So here we are. You are with him and I am still here, trying to make sense of it all.

I now am left with the realization that the next time I hold you in my arms will not be on this Earth but the day I meet you at heaven's door. I still wish I could bargain with him. I know that God has the ability to change the master plan, to roll the stone away, but I would never ask for you to come back to the sadness of this place. You are where you should be. I just wish I could have been your mother as I had wished for.

It's strange because I know he CALLED me to be your mother. I have wondered what that charge means if you are not here with me. I am starting to realize and am fully aware that my job now is to share with the world the beauty I found in your eyes, to make sure everyone knows your name and that your life is counted. That is my job as your mother. So I will carry you not only in my heart but also on my sleeve. You will go where I go and your life will change the world because you first changed me.

One day, when my time here has finished, I will meet my maker, my creator, and I hope he will have you there with him. I hope he will pass you from his arms to mine. I promise I will be the mommy you always deserved. I will never let you go. Once I get there, we will have tea parties and dress in beautiful dresses. We will bake cupcakes and read fairytales. You can comb my hair, and I'll paint your toenails. I will tuck you in bed every night and sing you a lullaby. Daddy will push you on the swings and we will sail away together on that crystal sea.

It won't be long. I'll be there before you know it. It will be easy to see me coming. You'll know me by the smile I will be wearing on my face. It will be the brightest one by far.

Wait for me at the gate my sweet Adama, for I love you so.

Love,
Mommy

I finished the letter just as the car came to a stop.

I quickly stuffed my notebook down into my bag and pulled every bit of myself together that I could. I smoothed my hair back into a sleek ponytail, as though that would somehow make me appear to be in one piece, unaffected, and still standing.

We climbed the stairs to the office we were told would house all death certificates. The hallway was filled with people sitting around and sleeping on the floor. I *still* don't know why. It was so strange the way so many were congregating outside the office. We walked in and my mouth hit the floor.

An entire wall was filled with files. Hundreds stacked high. There was no filing cabinet. They were just stacked in heaps. What caused my heart to stop, however, was that most of the files were charred and burned. I don't know if they had a random fire in that office or if they were retrieved during the war when the offices were set ablaze during the riots. Either way, I have *no idea* how you would ever locate the file on a particular person. I could see no rhyme or reason to the madness. I began to lose hope.

The man behind the desk looked up at me as we walked in, and I could tell he was not thrilled to see me. He mumbled under his breath and asked what I was there for.

I told him that I had guardianship of a child living in an orphanage on the east side. I told him that she had recently passed and I assumed her death was recorded here in his office somewhere. I asked him if he could check and that I would like a copy of the file for my records. It went downhill from there.

We do not have recent deaths recorded. Not to mention the hospitals do not report the deaths. The family reports and files the death. So, I am sorry but I cannot help you.

Okay. I took a deep breath and counted to five. I wanted to smack him in the face. He was so damn cynical and hateful and unfeeling. I realized that in order to make Adama's life count, in order to not leave her as a statistic, I would have to file her death myself. But I couldn't without a medical report. So again, I needed to get to that hospital and find the doctor who was on duty the night Adama died. My only option was to show up and just start asking around.

So that's exactly what we did next.

7.

WHEN GOOD NEWS BECOMES BAD NEWS
2004

It is not despair, for despair is only for those who see the end beyond all doubt. We do not.
—JRR Tolkien, *The Fellowship of the Ring*

The day we got the call will be etched in my mind for the rest of my life.

I decided to go into work early that morning. I wanted to take a few days off, so I was trying to catch up on everything that was on my desk, hoping to leave without a plateful sitting there once I got back.

My cell phone started ringing, and I noticed it was a

California number. It was *the* California number. Our agency was calling my phone and they never call me. EVER.

I answered the call and held my breath. What followed is now a blur. All I can really remember hearing was that we had been granted a court order —Jayda was now officially our daughter. It was time to book plane tickets and apply for her visa. I felt my heart come out of my chest. Tears came like a flood, and I ran straight for my car and headed to the church to find Jason.

That night Jason and I began calling family members and friends, telling them all the news. I think most people were in shock. I know we were. It felt as though 10,000 pounds had been lifted from my chest. I immediately went into nesting mode again. By this time Jayda was five years old. More than three years had gone by. I was collecting new clothes and shoes. I took several trips to the toy store to buy everything I thought a little girl would love. I was spoiling her rotten and she wasn't even here yet.

I spent those next few nights lying in bed envisioning what it would be like bringing her home. I also thought a lot about our son Jordan. I knew that being an only child and then all of a sudden having this kid show up who is supposed to be your sister but looks nothing like you wouldn't be easy. I knew Jayda also spoke little to no English. We would have our hands full. Having our hands full had been the gift I had been waiting for, wishing for, pleading for. God had finally shown up. He spread a bit of light into the dark, and I knew that the end was near. Or maybe better yet, the beginning was just up ahead.

About two weeks later, as we continued preparing for Jayda's homecoming, we were dealt a blow I could have never imagined. I was once again sitting at my desk when my phone rang. I was on another line with a client so I couldn't answer it, but I noticed that the number was restricted. That was odd to me so I tied up my conversation as quickly as possible, grabbed my phone and headed to the bathroom, the only quiet place I could find, to listen to the message.

The woman's voicemail stated she was with the U.S. State Department. She asked me to contact her as soon as possible concerning my pending adoption case at the embassy in Dakar. Under normal circumstances, I would have been excited to hear news about our adoption, but the tone in this woman's voice sent chills down my spine. She didn't sound like she was calling me to give me good news. She sounded cold and collected with a bit of sadness in her voice. It took me a few minutes to calm my nerves before I could dial the number.

Once I got through, I was placed on hold for what seemed like an eternity. Eventually the same woman who had left the message answered the phone. It turns out I was actually speaking with the head consular of the U.S. Embassy in Dakar, Senegal. This didn't help my nerves one bit.

She began by telling me that she understood we had been in a very long adoption process, had recently received our court order, and had filed a petition for an immigrant visa. She asked if that was all accurate. I told her it was accurate and that we had just been contacted by our agency a few weeks prior with the news. She hesitated, and, after a long pause that felt like eternity, she began to tell me what would rock me to my core.

After investigating your case we have come to the conclusion that your case is fraudulent. Your agency has participated in fraudulent practices within the country of Sierra Leone. They processed a bogus court order. You never went to court.

Silence.

Ma'am, are you still there?

Yes. I'm here. I just… I just don't think I understand.

Ma'am, I know this is very difficult, but I need you to understand this office is unable to process your petition. It has been denied. Due to the allegations against your agency, and the trafficking scandal within the country, it is impossible for you to go to court, get a valid court order, and get her out of that country.

I stammered.

So, now what? What do we do?

With a sad but frank tone she said,

Ma'am, my advice would be for you to grieve your daughter and move on to another country, one that can process a successful adoption on your behalf. Good luck and, again, I am very sorry you have been put through such a terrible loss.

I don't remember hanging up. All I remember is falling apart.

◆ ◆ ◆

Jason took the call from the State Department as the white flag in our battle to bring Jayda home. In his mind we had tried everything. We had sold everything. It was evident to him that, for whatever reason, the door had closed on our adoption. It was time to move on. This caused my blood to boil. I felt like I no longer knew him, like we lived in the same home but were complete strangers. He was tired and worn down. I, on the other hand, was just getting started.

I couldn't accept it. I *wouldn't* accept it. Jayda is my daughter. What seemed like an impossible road would never change that for me. I was so tired of hearing people use "God's will" as their go-to phrase when talking through our struggles.

Whoever said God's will was easy? Whoever said that the road we walk will be filled with fields of flowers and communities of people surrounding us, singing Kumbaya?

Making a difference, shifting culture, standing up for those who are persecuted, abandoned, and exploited is what I call trench work. It's messy, dirty, and no one wants to be there — in the middle of it all — because it's hard. And that's a fact. It's dirty, it's dark, and it exposes the underbelly of our society. People would rather pretend a closed door means God said no. It gets them out of the responsibility of doing the hard thing. I couldn't take it anymore. I decided that I wouldn't stop until my daughter came home. I didn't know what that meant, but I knew that I couldn't leave her. I could not forsake her. We were all she had. Who else would go to the other side of the world for her if we wouldn't?

The wall between Jason and me continued to grow. I felt like finding our way back to each other might not ever happen. The harder I pushed, the stronger he stood against it. I started to feel that if anyone would be responsible for keeping me from our daughter, in the end, it would be him. I didn't know how to live with that.

It was heartbreaking how the situation we were in had has such a way of twisting our lives and creating the illusion that we are against one another, that it was me against him. I felt like we were about to fall hard this time and we wouldn't get back up.

We hadn't spoken about Jayda for several weeks. During the silence I kept researching ways to get to her, how to beat the system. The problem was there were so few adoptions in Sierra Leone, finding a path was next to impossible.

Eventually I came across an online group and connected to a few other families that were also adopting through the same agency. After hearing they were attempting to travel, I knew it was time to take that same step and cross the ocean. I was ready to go. I was ready to sweep Jayda up into my arms, but I knew that I may be going alone. That was something I wasn't ready for.

I waited two more days before I approached Jason about the possibility of traveling to find Jayda and attempting to apply for court independently. What made this even harder to discuss was the fact that we were in the thick of the war between the U.S. and Iraq and Afghanistan. Americans were being beheaded. Sierra Leone supposedly had links to Al Qaeda. There were travel warnings for the country of Sierra Leone — the U.S. State Department was requesting that no Americans travel into the country unless it was an emergency. In my mind, this was an emergency.

When I finally sat down to talk to Jason about my idea, I could tell it was not going to go well. As I dug into all my reasons why, I could see him shutting down. I knew he thought I was crazy. I knew he just wanted to breathe. He was so tired. I think in his mind he was grieving a daughter, and, by letting go, one day we would be able to start over again and move on.

What followed was one of the hardest nights we had ever faced as a couple. He wasn't budging, and neither was I. So where did that leave us? I knew that fighting against one another wasn't the right move, but I also knew we couldn't quit.

I ran upstairs in a crying fit of grief, sadness, rage, and frustration. I was sobbing and vacuuming the upstairs bonus room when he walked in. He looked beat down, and I could tell he had been crying. He went on to tell me that if it were Jordan, no one would keep him from his son. He knew he had been called to be Jayda's father and he had to treat her with that same devotion as he would our natural born son. He said that he felt like we really needed to go. It was clear he didn't want to go, but I could see all over his face and in his body language he was submitting to the crazy plan. He cried, and I cried. That night was the first night in quite some time that I felt his arms around me and I didn't want him to ever let me go. I had missed him. I had missed us so much.

Once we made the decision to go to Sierra Leone to find Jayda, hand in hand we stood united, and told our parents. We knew we would face great opposition from our family. And we did. To say they were upset would be an understatement.

We've only felt like we disappointed our parents a few times in our lives. Growing up, I only found myself in a screaming match with my dad a handful of times. This was one of those times.

It was so hard to understand why they wouldn't accept and support us getting on that plane to go find our daughter and to fight for her. Jason's parents just wanted the whole thing to be over. They could not wrap their minds around the adoption in the first place, and now they felt we had chosen one child over the other. They felt like we were leaving Jordan to go into a dangerous country and were putting his needs second. In their minds, I really think Jayda was just another child, a statistic. They had not yet accepted her. I don't blame them. I know how hard it is for some, and Jason's parents were no exception.

My parents were equally upset, though my mom was a little more understanding. I had emptied my heart out to her so many times leading up to this decision. She knew it was a greater calling and we had been chosen to do this. We had said yes to adoption, and she supported us. My dad wasn't happy at all. He couldn't understand why I would get on a plane and land in a country recovering from a brutal civil war. He just couldn't understand that risk. I was his daughter, and he was scared.

Once we booked our tickets the real stress began. We

began getting calls from the agency telling us that it was a mistake to travel. They told us that we would not be allowed to see our daughter without permission. They wouldn't tell us how to find her or what steps to take once we arrived. The embassy even reached out to us once we had registered our trip online. They highly suggested we cancel our travel plans.

Everywhere we turned there were bright red warning signs, cautioning us that we were going the wrong way, that we needed to turn around. For me, it was just confirmation we were meant to go. I knew we were in a season of battle and the war was about to get nasty. We were fighting for a child after all, a child who had been orphaned.

Bring on that plane. We were ready. Or so I thought.

8.

THE FACTS
2011

The terrible thing about the quest for
truth is that you find it.
— Remy de Gourmont

The urgency I felt when hopping that plane to Sierra Leone during my quest to find Jayda felt eerily similar to the urgency I felt now. The answers I needed surrounding Adama's death would be salve to my heart. Yes, it wouldn't fix anything. But I had to know. I had to find the truth. So, I became that same bull in a china cabinet that I had become so many years before. If only that woman had never left the building, how things might be different now.

It probably took about two hours to get to the hospital from town. It felt like it took three solid days. The morning had already been so long and uninviting. It felt like we were pushing against what should be, like the day was not at all happy with our plans. Everything was against us, including the traffic. Unless you've witnessed it firsthand there is no describing the bumper-to-bumper chaos that exists in Freetown. Drained from that frustration and overwhelmed by the thoughts running through my brain, I was just ready to get there. The hospital was on the far end of the east side of the city, and when we pulled in I felt myself begin to fade fast. I wasn't sure if I could handle going inside. My mouth was dry. My heart was racing. My legs felt like they wouldn't be able to handle the task of walking me toward the entrance. I wanted to pass out. Yet, keeping it together was the only option.

As I stared at the entrance, I could almost see it all unfold before me. I knew my eyes were playing tricks on me. But it all seemed so real. I could see Adama being carried through those doors in the middle of the night. Swiftly and with force, the doors flying open. She was rushed inside, but by who? I still didn't know who had decided she needed medical attention. I still didn't know who was with her in those final moments. I could see her being carried with caution. Her body was limp, lethargic, breaking down second by second. I had to believe she wasn't in any pain. I couldn't accept it otherwise. I could imagine the shouting and the scurry of nurses making way for those who brought her in. I've thought about this, branding the picture in my mind, and revisiting it over and over again through the years. It became a fixture in my dreams after the fact. How I wished I'd been there. Accepting that I missed her last breath, that she likely laid alone on a gurney with no one to usher her through those last moments, makes everything inside me burn with fury.

As we walked toward the entrance and Osseh opened the doors, I snapped back to reality and took a deep breath. With purpose in my step, I focused on the breathing in and the breathing out. I moved toward the doors and went inside.

I began asking around. I asked to speak with the doctor on duty, assuming there were only a few who even worked there. I got in front of one, and I told him the story we were told. I remember his eyes were kind yet hollow. He looked tired and worn down, likely by the weight he carried. I am sure it felt like the world was on his shoulders. And here was this random white woman investigating a death that happened under his watch. I probably was not a welcomed visitor, but I was blind to all that. I only cared about one thing — the truth. The doctor seemed nervous but maintained his composure rather well. I began asking him if he remembered the little girl or if he knew who may have treated her that night.

He took a deep breath, letting out a sigh. I could tell

he knew *exactly* who I was talking about. He shook his head and confirmed the story. Yes, she had come into the emergency room unresponsive but still alive. He said she only lasted a few hours before she took her last breath. I asked him what would cause her to decline so rapidly if she had been cared for and was taking meds. He confirmed to me he had never seen her before that night and couldn't say for sure if she had been on meds or not. I believe he felt she had not been properly cared for leading up to her arrival, but he wouldn't throw Ina under the bus. Over and over again he said,

It was a very unfortunate situation. If only they had brought her here sooner.

I could see the sorrow in his eyes as he recalled that night, and I wanted to hug him for it. He was the first bystander who seemed to care at all about what happened to Adama. I could see he felt nervous to say too much to me. After all, I was the adoptive parent, and I was an American woman with a dead child on her hands. I am sure I was viewed as a ticking bomb. One wrong move and I would detonate. And I think they would have been right.

He carefully danced around certain questions. But in his eyes, I knew he knew the truth. They were neglecting her in her final days. She didn't just suddenly fall ill. Her brain hemorrhage came after days, if not weeks and months, of neglect. The doctor was as disturbed as I was. He continued to give his condolences, interjecting "I'm so sorry" as often as he could. Beads of sweat pooled on his brow — not necessarily because he was nervous. Maybe because the weight of the situation caused his body as much stress as it did mine. I felt a sense of solidarity with this man. He was doing the best he could. But his best didn't change the reality. Death was imminent. The hope to save who he could, knowing he would bury most, was all dark, ugly, and sad. Unfortunately, he was stuck in the middle of it all.

I eventually conjured up the nerve to ask him for a copy of the medical report. I told him I wanted to give Adama a proper burial and also to make sure her death was recorded publicly. He kindly made a copy. As I stared down at the paper in my hands, I couldn't decide if I was holding gold or my biggest nightmare. I suppose it was a little of both. I held tightly to the report, as though the entire world was in those papers, and left the hospital.

Next stop: the death certificate office. Now that I had the proper paperwork, I wanted to get back today before they closed. Supposedly her grave was nearby, but I couldn't face that just yet. I needed to make more headway first. I just wasn't ready for what I would see. The reality and finality of it all. I knew it would break me and I wasn't ready to shatter just yet. So, I continued stuffing down the truth and kept moving forward, one foot in front of the other.

The offices were close to shutting down for the day. I

knew those working inside are always counting down to closing time. Many were probably already long gone. I raced up the steps and turned the corner where nothing much had changed since we had been there hours before. People were still sleeping and lingering down the halls. I quickly made my way through the maze of people and went inside. Of course, the man who should have been sitting behind the desk wasn't there. So, we waited. And waited. And waited some more. Finally, he came back, seemingly in a hurry and clearly agitated I was back so soon.

I told him I had visited the hospital, spoken to the doctor, and was given a copy of the medical report. He seemed very surprised and his agitation grew. He took it from my hands and looked over it for a bit. Then looking up at me he said,

So. Who are you to this child?

As if he didn't know. We had already been through all of this.

I told him I was the adoptive parent. Explained the situation *again*, just as I had during my first visit that morning. He wanted proof. So, I pulled out my court paperwork and showed him our papers.

Ma'am, we do not create death certificates for orphans. I'm sorry. Your court order has not been granted yet so she technically was not a child with parents. She is an orphan.

I took a breath and started counting under my breath.

I felt the heat slowly rising in my face. I could feel myself losing all control, and there was nothing I could do about it.

What do you mean you don't create death certificates for orphans? What does her parental status have to do with ANYTHING? She died. Her death should be recorded! That's the job of this office. To accurately track and report the number of deaths in Sierra Leone. She should be among those reported!

He then handed me back my paperwork, turned his seat back toward his desk, and, with his back to me, said,

As I said, orphans are statistics only and not counted in our recording of deaths in Sierra Leone. And if I DID decide to record her death for you, well…. you would have to show me proof she was dead.

PROOF? PROOF she was DEAD?

I was so angry I couldn't see. Tears were brimming, and I felt the mother of all meltdowns about to unload on this man.

I'm sorry sir, HOW WOULD I PROVE HER DEATH TO YOU? You want me to bring her dead body back here in my backpack?! Dig her up and snap pictures of a decomposed body!?

One of the Americans traveling with us placed her hand on my shoulder in an effort to quiet me down. People were starting to congregate to see what the screaming was all about.

DON'T touch me!

I angrily stepped away from her and leaned in closer to the man.

You are telling me that this child means so little to this country that she won't even be counted among you in DEATH!?

I began sobbing. I pulled out my billfold and started handing him money.

THIS IS INSANE! HERE! Is this what you want? What's it gonna take? $100? $200? $500? TAKE IT! Just give me the death certificate! NOW!

I was sweating, sobbing, screaming. People were whispering. Osseh looked mortified. And of course — the man took the money. Just as I knew he would.

Within minutes, I had a death certificate. Proving Adama had lived — and died. It meant nothing to the rest of the world, but it mattered to me. It was a small victory, and it mattered.

9.

THE BURIAL
2011

Grief is just love with no place to go.
—Jamie Anderson

I don't recall anything else that happened between that last visit to the office and standing at Adama's makeshift grave on the side of the highway. I can't tell you if it was the same day or the next day. I can't even tell you how I got there. I don't remember who traveled with me. All I know is that, at some point, Osseh and I made the journey across town once again.

Osseh — what a fixture, a foundation in my life. He had been my rock through so many dark seasons, through so many groundbreaking moments. I'm sure if you asked him, he would wish otherwise. That we had never met. But we did, and I stuck to him like glue. He was honest, a brother to me in so many ways. I pulled him into so many crazy situations over the years. Here we were again. Walking a road not yet traveled. We were used to fighting the good fight, raising hell where we could to take out injustice, and in most cases, we won. But this time we were maneuvering loss. We were saying goodbye.

We pulled into an alley, right off the highway that connects the east side of town to downtown Freetown. I can remember getting out of the car and closing my eyes. The pain in my chest was so intense I felt like I was holding on to my life with every breath. I wondered if it was a heart attack or just anxiety. I didn't know, but it hurt like hell. So, I kept my eyes closed and continued to breathe, just as I had done since I got the news. I was taking everything in, then exhaling it all, one moment at a time.

Osseh stepped away for a few minutes. He was asking around, trying to find someone who may have information as to where exactly Adama had been buried. While he was gone, I began wandering around. The area was supposed to be a cemetery of some sort. There were a few cement-enclosed burials here and there, but mostly I just saw mounds of dirt piled high as though someone had just dumped a load from a wheelbarrow. You would think the dirt piles would at least be lined neatly in rows, but that wasn't the case. The graves were sporadic, almost like people just pulled up to the area with bodies in tow, picked a spot that looked good to them, and just started digging.

I walked back toward the car and rested on the bumper. My legs felt heavy, and I was so dizzy. The heat was unbearable. I wanted to go home — a familiar feeling. The urge to run had hit me many times before.

Before long, Osseh came back. He was following behind a man who seemed intent and focused on the mission at hand. He walked past me swiftly, not even noticing I was there, and headed toward the burial mounds. He looked around for a bit and then pointed to a fresh pile of dirt. Osseh waved me over.

I realized I needed to step up. I needed to start moving, but I couldn't. If you've never felt time freeze, be glad. It's scary. To know your world is crashing down around you, and there is nothing you can do about it. Thinking if you choose to not participate somehow the pain will all go away. But it doesn't. It all breaks down whether we are ready or not. Slowly, I began moving toward him, forcing my legs to work. It felt like they were fighting me, refusing to take me to the pain that was coming next. I crossed the road and made my way to both of them. As I approached, Osseh told me in a quiet whisper that this was the place Adama had been buried.

The pile of dirt was smaller than most others in the area. You could tell a very small body lay underneath. There was nothing that marked the grave. There were no flowers, not even a simple stone to set her apart. Just dirt. You'd think the tears would have begun flowing at this point. The moment was sobering, numbing, hard to swallow and accept. But the tears didn't come. I only felt numb. It all seemed so matter-of-fact. I slowly allowed my knees to finally buckle underneath me and made my way to the ground. I sat next to the dirt and began pulling the weeds growing up from underneath it. It angered me how her grave was left unattended and neglected. Just as she had been while she was alive. Neglected. I shouldn't have been surprised. I didn't notice right away, but several people had gathered around. Despite the crowd, I still felt very much alone. It was in that moment I began talking to the God who had left my daughter. I had ignored him since I found out. Yes, I was giving God the silent treatment like a spoiled teenager. Up till now I had nothing to say to him. In my mind he had held all the cards, the keys to unlocking Adama from the prison she lived in. And he didn't. He failed me. He failed her. I trusted he would bring her home to me, and he didn't come through. As I sat there smoothing the dirt, picking up handfuls and watching it slip through my fingers just as Adama had, I began to think back.

We had tried so hard to rescue the kids at Ina's orphanage. No stone was left unturned. Our complaints and pleas for intervention hit every office and ministry only to fall on deaf ears. Our voices took center stage even before the president's office, and still no action was taken to protect those children. Adama, as young and fragile as she was, was a sitting duck. I started thinking about how maybe God did act on her behalf. He brought me into her life. It was my responsibility to stay mobilized until she was free. Instead, I took a step back and chose to open a center instead, thinking I had time, thinking that eventually I would find the right opportunity to get her out. I should have never laid my gun down in the battle. I should have never given them ground. They took it. I realized that my big mouth brought visibility to Adama's crisis yet no one else acted on her behalf. Her blood was on all of us. Indifference costs lives. Refusing to take swift, immediate action results in the death of children hanging in the balance. It wasn't God who let me down. I let him down. I failed.

At that moment I felt like I saw Jesus or maybe I just really wanted to believe he was there with me in that moment, telling me the truth. I could see him kneeling just across from me on the other side of the grave, body bent over where Adama lay with his arms outstretched. When he lifted himself off the grave, in his arms was my little girl. He took charge. He did what he had to do. He knew the government would never step in on her behalf and do the right thing. He knew I would never give in to the bribe. He knew those running Ina's orphanage would only continue to neglect and harbor her. She would remain a victim, a statistic, a pawn in a cruel game. So, he took her back. Just like that.

I want to believe that. I want to believe he was there that day. I want to believe he just took her, to rescue her from the atrocities she was forced to endure. But part of me thinks, it is what it is. Adama's death wasn't a grand gesture by God, rescuing her from her captors. It was a fact of life.

I continue to question myself, wondering why I hadn't fought for her the way I had fought for Jayda so many years before. What had happened to me? Where had my stamina gone? Why was it so easy for me to lie down and let them take her from me? When I was fighting for Jayda, they would have had to kill me first.

10.

CROSSING THE WATER
2004

Courage is being scared to death, and saddling up anyway.
—John Wayne

Boarding that plane for Sierra Leone felt every bit like an out-of-body experience. I was barely 25 years old, naive and hopeful and also scared and filled with intense dread. As the flight attendant's voice came over the intercom, the whole world seemed to slow down. The conversations surrounding us turned into a quiet hum, echoing in time with the airplane engines. I could feel and hear the air come into my lungs and escape back out with every breath I took. Counting to ten, closing my eyes, I started thinking back on the previous day when I said goodbye to Jordan.

I took him to my parent's house to stay while we were away. I had told him time and time again why we were leaving and how long we would be gone, but for God's sake, he was only five years old. All he knew was that we were leaving, and the goodbye truly felt like it may be one of my last memories of him. As I held him in my arms, I buried my face into his neck and kissed him through my tears. I tried so hard not to let him see, but soon the tears brought a tidal wave of emotion. I felt like my chest would explode any second. Every caution and concern thrown at us over the last few weeks came back into my mind, and I wondered if we really were crazy. We were getting ready to fly thousands of miles across the world, into a war-ravaged nation, with no plan in place, hoping to find a child we had already been told could never leave the country. What were we thinking? Was I walking away from one child to try to save another? Had I crossed the line? If something happened to us, would Jordan ever forgive us? Would he ever understand the passion and cause behind our decision to go? Would he think we had chosen a calling over him? Or would self-sacrifice be the one lesson he would learn from his parents? To live with purpose — would that ignite his bones if he lived the rest of his life without us?

The final call to fasten our seatbelt jolted me back to the present, and I looked over to see Jason staring out the window wearing that same mask of fear. I grabbed his hand, thankful we were finally in this together.

The flights were daunting. Jason and I had never traveled internationally so we were trying everything we could to hold ourselves together as we landed in Belgium, switched planes, and prepared for the last flight to Freetown. Thankfully we had a few other travelers with us. We had joined arms with a Methodist mission team that had traveled many times before. Our plan was to follow them into the country and blend in as best we could.

After about 24 hours of flying it was time to land. Fear got the best of me, and I could feel tears brimming. For a split second I wanted to turn around and go right back home to everything I had left behind. What if this trip turned into a disaster? What if we never find Jayda? What if we find ourselves in a scandal? What if? What if? What if?

The plane door opened and immediately people started grabbing their luggage and departing the plane. There was no turning back. We were about to step foot onto African soil. Little did I know we were preparing to press our feet into the dirt of what would become our second home.

Exiting the plane was my first reality check, proof I wasn't in a dream, but that we actually really had just traveled across the world.

The smell, the humidity, the darkness was all so overwhelming. There were so many people everywhere. The culture shock almost took the air right out of my lungs. I felt so vulnerable. Masses of people began to congregate around us, trying to take our bags, asking for money. Scads of people were shouting over one another trying to get our attention. I wanted to crawl into a hole and die right there on the spot. Within about five minutes I was drenched in sweat and felt like I would throw up at any moment.

You could tell within minutes of landing that the country was in shambles. The airport was terribly chaotic and it felt as though we were in a fire drill of sorts. There was no order to anything. We were pushed from one line to the next until we found ourselves leaving the airport and walking down a dark dirt path behind the building. I had no idea where we were going, and we were too afraid to ask any questions. Thankfully we were tagging along with the mission team so at least we felt part of a group. I honestly don't know how we would have managed without them on that first trip.

We were led into a metal outbuilding. I immediately noticed the effects of war. Bullet holes riddled the walls. We were told by airport officials to sit down on nearby benches and wait. We were then told we had another flight to catch — a helicopter to be exact. I finally realized we were not actually in Freetown yet. We had landed on the other side of the water and had to cross it to get to the city.

We waited for hours before it was finally our turn. We filed in line and headed to the helipad. It was an army chopper. I couldn't believe it. I felt like I was living someone else's life. I didn't know whether to laugh or cry. We climbed into the aircraft and found our luggage stacked up in the center. We were told to find a place to sit along the side and if there was a seatbelt available, to fasten it. Yes, you read that right. Not everyone had a seatbelt.

As the helicopter started its engine, I felt so much fear rise up within my chest I began to feel lightheaded. I had never fainted in my life but this would be as good a time as any to give it a try.

I began counting to ten again, held Jason's hands as tightly as I could, and squeezed my eyes shut. It was so dark outside, and truly that was a blessing. As we crossed the water, we were told the flight would last about eight minutes. Those eight minutes felt like three hours. As we began the descent, I was surprised to see that most of the city was in the dark. There was no sign of electricity. The entire area was immersed in complete darkness. I would soon learn exactly what being in an undeveloped country meant.

As we climbed out of the helicopter, I waited on my eyes to adjust to the darkness around me. As my surroundings came into focus, I realized I was about to come undone. There was a deep cry rising in my throat, and I knew I couldn't let it out. So it pulsated and ached from the inside. Fighting tears, I swallowed hard and tried to remember what my youth pastor had told me years before.

Don't miss the divine appointments, the invitation.

I decided right then and there that I would become a sponge. I would take it all in and prepare myself for the fact that I would never be the same.

My first few hours in Sierra Leone are neatly packed away in my mind. I have kept the memories there for safekeeping, knowing that — for me — that was my first step into the battle against injustice. It was the first chance I ever had to actually recognize it and react to it. I was bombarded by the reality of war and survival as soon as we hit the ground.

I thought I understood the devastation of war. I had studied it in school, but I had never seen the effects first-hand. I had never been immersed in the aftermath of war until now.

I noticed immediately that a large number of the beggars in the streets were amputees. My mind took a snapshot of the amputee refugee camp we passed as we made our way into the city. I lost count of the number of UN vehicles we passed. It was unnerving to realize that the country was so very fragile. They still needed peacekeeping troops. It was common to see groups of military personnel in the middle of town sitting on the backs of trucks, holding machine guns. Seeing it all with my own eyes made me feel like I was in the middle of a bad dream. But it was truly a nightmare for those who had just lived through it. A real-life horror story, and the people of this country had been the main characters, the victims of atrocities I could not begin to wrap my mind around.

We eventually made it to the home of a missionary family we had connected with prior to our trip. They allowed us to stay with them during our time in-country. It was a breath of fresh air to meet someone who understood our fears and could walk us through the uncertainties we would face in the days to come. The family had stew and hot bread waiting for us, and a bed calling our names. As we settled in on that first night it was hard to find sleep. My head wouldn't stay quiet. Neither would Jason's. We tossed and turned while our minds played a tennis match. Back and forth with all our questions and fears. It felt like chaos, like a riot in the brain. Eventually the whirring of the fans in the room carried us off into a sleep, and I dreamed about Jayda as I had so many times before. But this time it was different. This time we were on the same side of the ocean for the very first time.

11.

BLOW BY BLOW
2004

*So, I love you because the entire universe
conspired to help me find you.*
—Paul Coelho, *The Alchemist*

As the sun rose early that October morning, I didn't have a difficult time rising for the occasion. In just a few short hours we would visit the center where Jayda was living. All I could think about was scooping her up into my arms. My heart was beating out of my chest with excitement. I had waited so long for this moment. We had a pretty good idea of where the orphanage sat within the city of Freetown.

We loaded up Osseh's van and started a steep climb up the hill to a main street in the middle of town. It was my first time experiencing the streets of Freetown. I was shocked at how many people crowded the streets and the number of cars driving bumper to bumper. There seemed to be no traffic flow, no rules, and it was a little nerve-wracking. Horns honking from every direction, street children flocking the vehicle looking for food or for change. Our brains were overloaded with what we were witnessing, and we were weighed down by emotion we didn't know what to do with. I kept watching the street children and envisioning my little girl. Would that be her fate? Would she be one of them without adoption? What would her future be like if we were not successful in our plight? I couldn't go there. I continued to hold onto the voice in my head telling my heart that *this* was supposed to be. A way would be made. A door would open. I wanted to believe she was always meant to be my daughter. So I held on to that belief and refused to think about any other option.

We rounded the bend and began descending down a steep dirt road. I wasn't sure if the van would make it down the hill, let alone back up it. There were more potholes than there was road. It was incredible how skilled Osseh was in maneuvering the vehicle just so to avoid losing a tire or worse. We turned the corner, and ahead of us was a giant concrete wall with a large gate at the center. Osseh told us that he was pretty sure this was the place. He began to honk his horn and slowly the gates opened. My heart quickened. A young man came out and stood at the window of the car. We told him who we were and why we were there. He went back inside for a few minutes and we got a little nervous thinking that he may not let us inside. Once he returned, he waved us in and opened the gates to make room for the vehicle to enter.

We got out of the van and several more staff members were waiting at the door of the center to welcome us inside. It seemed too easy. Again, my heart was pounding so fast it was all I could hear inside my head. I was shaking as we walked through the doors, knowing within moments I would be united after so many years with the child I had prayed for.

We made our way through the dark entryway and were ushered into a "waiting room."

The waiting room was so familiar to me. Every photograph we had ever received of our daughter had been taken in that room. We sat on pins and needles, holding presents in our hands and hope in our hearts. We were overflowing from the inside out.

We heard commotion outside, and, before I even realized what was happening, in walked a group of staff members. From behind the back of a skirted African woman emerged a tiny child.

My child.

She was stunning. Captivating. She was more beautiful than the pictures I had kept neatly in a box for safekeeping. She was more beautiful than I remembered her being in the dreams I had of her over the past four years. She was standing before me in living color. It had been such a long season of waiting, yet in that moment it felt as though she and I had never been apart. It felt as though she had always been mine and not this itty-bitty stranger standing in front of me. I wanted so badly to pick her up and to run, to run as fast as I could away from the injustice we had been fighting, away from all the red tape and all the controversy. If we could just run and hide away that would be perfect. If we could find someplace where the world was right, where little girls would no longer be orphaned, and families could just be family. I looked at her and for a brief moment I couldn't believe we had actually made it this far. How did we end up here, on the other side of the world? And then as quickly as I forgot how we landed in this place, the memories came flooding back. This had been war, and we had not been left unscathed. In fact, our fight was only beginning.

We were allowed to take Jayda with us so we holed away at a guest house, and we built a plan to get her adoption through court. Those few weeks were hell for us. We felt as though we were standing in a dark hallway. In that dark hallway were 10,000 doors. Each door seemed inviting at first. We would approach, knock, and wait. When it wouldn't open, we would push. Hard. But you see these doors were made of iron and steel, calloused and stronger than we were. Pushing wore us down, and the doors remained closed, locked from the inside. You see there were no keys that could open them. It was always someone else deciding whether or not to open the doors and welcome us in.

We found ourselves fighting to be heard, begging and pleading for mercy on our case. The HANCI trafficking scandal in Sierra Leone was all over the news, in all the papers, and every time we would approach someone with our daughter in hand, we were immediately under scrutiny. The assumption was that we were also traffickers. Anytime the door opened just a crack, it would slam in our faces again when they saw us, the color of our skin, and realized our intent was to take a child out of Sierra Leone. We found ourselves back at square one over and over again.

We finally came across an attorney who told us he held the key to the door we needed to open. He guaranteed us that he could get us an adoption order and get us all out of the country within a week. We were fools enough to believe him. We paid him and he "got to work." It wasn't easy like he said it would be. It was downright impossible.

He started his process by setting a meeting with the Ministry of Social Welfare where we shared our intent to adopt Jayda. We quickly came to realize the approval to proceed to court was in the hands of this specific office. And that approval wouldn't come easy.

I could tell the staff was trying to handle us very carefully, as if we were grenades they were trying to avoid detonating. We knew they didn't want to approve our petition to proceed to court, but they decided to take us through the process and determine if Jayda's birth family was aware of and open to her adoption.

This was a *big* problem. The orphanage had not heard from Jayda's birthmother since she was abandoned. We had no idea where she was or if she was alive, but in order to proceed, it was made clear we had to find her. To avoid our case being viewed as child trafficking, she would have to approve the adoption. They assumed we would never find her. I assumed they were probably right.

We sent a woman who worked for the orphanage out to the refugee camp where Jayda was born, in hopes she would come across someone who would know where she was. We knew it was a long shot, a needle in a haystack, but we had to try. Our next appointment with social welfare was less than 24 hours away. If the birthmother was not present, our case would be dismissed.

Needless to say, we didn't sleep that night.

The next morning, we made our way once again through the chaotic traffic. We tried to settle our hearts, not knowing what we would find when we got to the ministry.

We arrived and sat in the waiting area for hours. We were told our turn was going to be soon. We felt like the world was crashing down on us. There had been no sign of Jayda's birthmother, and we knew without her we could not move forward.

I sat in the stifling heat with Jayda sleeping on my chest. She could sleep anywhere. She had been attached to me like another body part. I could feel her heart beating in time with mine, and I felt a cry begin to rise in my throat. Surely God would not bring me across the world to send her back to the orphanage. Surely this door would not slam in our faces.

I kissed her head and tasted the sweat across her forehead. I traced her brow with my fingers, trying to memorize her face. Twisting her curls and imagining that we were home, snuggled in her bed telling bedtime stories. All of a sudden we heard a commotion outside. The next thing I knew a young woman made her way into the room. She looked hesitant and scared, carrying a baby on her back — a spitting image of the child I was holding in my arms.

It was her.

My world stopped for a moment. I was about to come face to face with Jayda's birthmother. I wasn't ready. I had never been more frightened in my life. As she made her way toward me, I found my hands gripping Jayda's tiny body even harder as fear began to wrap itself around me.

She had not seen her child in several years. Would she change her mind? Would she want her back? I had in my arms my whole entire world, and I realized that in an instant it could be taken from me.

I forced a smile and tears begin to fall, not out of happiness that she had arrived, but, honestly, out of fear that she would take Jayda away.

I walked over to her and said hello. She didn't speak English, so a hug would have to do. I leaned in to hug her and what I thought would be an awkward embrace was anything but that. She held onto me like I was a life raft and she was drowning. Her smile was so big it lit up the whole room. Why was she so happy to see me? Why did she seem to love me, someone she didn't even know? I was asking to take her child away. I expected to feel like there was an ocean between us, when truly, to her, we were the rescue boat. I find travesty in this statement even as I write it. I didn't want to be a rescue boat. The fact that this even had to happen seemed unacceptable to me. I didn't want to have to save this child. I didn't want to have to take her from her mother.

Jayda was scared of her mother, and her mother honestly paid very little attention to the fact that her child was even in the room. It seemed so bizarre to me at the time. The disconnect was real. This mother had walked away, and it seemed as though she had no regrets about that.

While we continued to wait for the minister to meet with us, I watched as Jayda's mom walked from trashcan to trashcan searching for something. I wasn't sure what at first. She would pull out trash, dig around, and then eventually she pulled out the bones of fish someone had thrown away. She began pulling pieces of flesh from them, feeding it to the little one on her back. Then she would suck the bones dry, throw them back into the trash, and continue filtering through the rubbish.

She needed food.

I was sick. My heart was shattered in that moment, and I realized that she disconnected from her daughter because she had to. There was no option. This family was starving. She would save one by giving her to me, and she would fight to keep the other child alive until she found a rescue boat for him as well.

Finally, the minister called us into a conference room. The staff made it clear to all parties why we were there. Then the nightmare began. They began yelling and screaming at Jayda's birthmother like she was on trial. It was as if she had committed some unbelievable crime, and they were appalled and disgusted by her.

It was so hard to understand the full scope of the conversation since they were not speaking in English, but we were able to gather that they had publicly shamed her for abandoning her child. They threatened her, telling her she would likely never see the child again if she agreed to adoption, that they had no idea what might happen to her, and that she must make the decision.

The smile that had previously graced her face was gone. She sat in fear, tears streaming down her face. Then she began to get very angry. Before I knew it, Jayda's mother was yelling as loud as the rest of the room was yelling, and an employee from the orphanage took her aside and tried her best to calm her down. I could feel a loss of control over the situation and knew that at any moment she was going to grab Jayda out of my arms and storm out the door.

She eventually returned to the table. She was much calmer, and with a confidence in her voice she told the room she had abandoned Jayda years ago. She had no intentions of retrieving her due to her situation. The father was dead, and she wanted Jayda to be adopted and taken to America for a new life. The minister asked us to return the next day to pick up the letter of approval and then we would be free to proceed to court.

We left feeling 10,000 pounds lighter and yet weighed down with more hope than we could carry. We were ecstatic. Our next step was to convince a judge to hear our case and then to vote in our favor.

Over the next week we would attempt to be heard in court multiple times. Each time we would step in front of a judge we were denied. Every single time our case was handed down it would land in the lap of the same judge. Every time she would deny us without even hearing the case. She would rant about the trafficking scandal, the fact that we had not lived in-country for at least six months, and would just deny it. It was mind numbing and heartbreaking. I can remember during one particular session, we had just been denied. As the judge turned and exited the courtroom I broke down into tears. The clerk walked over to us and said that the judge felt bad for us. The judge knew we loved our daughter, but her hands were tied. Unless we could move to Sierra Leone and live there for at least six months, she couldn't help us. It was an impossible situation. As we left the courtroom, Jason collapsed onto the floor and sobbed. I had never seen him so broken. I felt so responsible for the pain he was feeling. I opened his eyes to this child. He fell in love, and now his heart was breaking into a million pieces because we were losing her. As he sat on the floor of the hallway, Jayda's grandfather slowly made his way to Jason's side. He reached down, placed his hand on Jason's shoulder and said, "She is your daughter. Nothing can change that. Have hope." Jason took the old man's hand and stood up to face him. They embraced, and it felt as though it had been decided in that moment. We were *not* giving up.

We were told that the problem was the chief justice who was in charge of handing down cases. He was handing our case down to the same judge on purpose, knowing she did not support adoption. He had no intention of seeing our case get approved given the negative adoption climate in Sierra Leone.

We decided we would simply request an appointment to meet with this chief justice and attempt to convince him to change his mind.

It didn't go well.

At all.

It's a day I'm not particularly proud of, a day I let the stress of the situation get to me. We had waited for hours to see him, and he wasn't letting us in. He seemed to enjoy making us wait all day long. I was very frustrated, especially after having a guard slam an AK47 into my chest because he didn't like what I was wearing into the courthouse that day. I had my fill of the back and forth, the ups and downs, and trying to maneuver through the lack of processes in a country that wasn't my own.

I called our attorney and asked him to come down to the courthouse to try to speak to the judge. He refused. I had a complete meltdown right then and there, on the steps of the courthouse, in front of the entire world. It was ugly. Very ugly.

We eventually did see the chief justice but to no avail. He would not support our cause and would not make us any promises to hand our case down to an impartial judge. He was arrogant. He smirked at us, and his office smelled like mildew and dead fish. I was over him and over the legalities of it all. As we continued filing and we continued to get denied, I began to lose hope.

Eventually we ran out of money — and out of time. We had no choice but to go home. We'd been fighting for nearly a month and had gained nothing.

Taking Jayda back to the orphanage was a memory that will forever be etched into my brain. It was like a deep wound, a scar that doesn't ever disappear.

The orphanage she lived in was a hellhole. Inside the walls were sadness, fear, dread, and little hope. Taking her back inside, leaving her, knowing she may never come home almost killed me. I felt as though I had taken her back inside a burning house and left her there, watching our hopes, our dreams and our little girl go up in smoke.

The flight home...well I can't actually remember it. I do remember the tears. The silent kind, the empty kind. The kind that, if spilled out, would overflow the deepest ocean.

12.

NIGHT ONLY LASTS SO LONG
2004

I will open a door that no man can shut.
—Revelation 3:8

Our house had never felt so empty. My heart had never felt so heavy. Her face invaded my sleep. It invaded every moment of every day. All I could think about was that look in her eyes when I turned and walked away from her that day. How final the goodbye had felt. How many times would this child have to experience loss? The scream she let out. The way her legs flailed in the arms of the caregiver. How they rushed her inside to try to avoid a disaster. The silent broken cry that filled her eyes as she screamed but no sound came out. I knew she couldn't handle much more, and neither could I.

I wrestled with God day and night. I couldn't wrap my brain around the why. Did everything really happen for a reason? You see this is what the community around us was saying. There was a "reason" for it all. I wasn't buying what they were selling. Their words didn't feel like salve to the soul. They felt like spit being spewed in my face, like salt in an open wound. Whoever thought words like that would make someone feel better when their world is caving in?

As it got closer to Thanksgiving, the gaping hole Jayda left behind became unbearable. Jason and I both felt we had to try again. We couldn't just lie down and quit. We couldn't leave her there. There had to be some way to get her out. Now that we had seen it all with our own eyes, we knew that her life would surely be snuffed out if left in the hands of those caring for her. Jayda would eventually end up in the streets or worse.

We decided to send Jason back on Thanksgiving Day. I would stay home with Jordan, and Jason would get back on a plane and try once again to get through court. We learned of an American attorney traveling to Sierra Leone at the same time. He had a clear understanding of the adoption laws in Sierra Leone. We allowed ourselves to feel hopeful again, that maybe this lawyer could help. The problem was we didn't have a dime to our name. We had spent every last cent on the previous trip. We had already taken out an equity loan against our home. We had no options but to literally not pay our bills that month. So that's what we did. We risked repossessions in an effort to try one last time to get Jayda home.

When Jason boarded the plane that day, he took my heart right along with him. The next few weeks passed over me like a violent storm. Every day I felt as though our lives were being turned inside out, like we were being pushed to the limit and soon would be completely undone. There were opposing forces at work trying everything they could to stop us from bringing Jayda home. Jason missed every flight that was scheduled. He ended up stuck in another African country, forced to travel on a plane that seemed to be from World War II, landed in a neighboring African country that refused to allow him to board his flight to Freetown unless he gave them all of his electronics as "payment." Let's just say that by the time he arrived in Sierra Leone he was spent, exhausted, and felt every bit defeated.

Here is where the story begins to get a bit hazy to me. It was such a blur that I have trouble getting it all out in order. I have to believe that God saw us in our distress. I think he was tired of watching us walk the hallway with locked doors at every turn. He stepped in and opened a door no man could close. After all, he had sent us this invitation, hadn't he? He was the one responsible for bringing Jayda into our lives. He had to show up to the party eventually, right?

Our case had been heard several more times via proxy before Jason ever actually arrived in-country. Each time it was denied. We knew it continued to get stuck with the chief justice. I've never prayed so hard for anything in my entire life. Eventually, the door swung open.

The morning came like any other. Jason preparing for court. Preparing for a day of begging and pleading with anyone who would listen. Newspapers hit the streets that morning with front-page news that interested us. The chief justice had been sacked. Fired. He had been immediately removed from office for reasons that were unclear. All we knew was that this was our chance. We filed again and lo and behold we got the *same* judge as each time before.

Jason called me.

It's over, Erica. They won't let us re-file, and our case was just handed down to the same judge again. I will call you after it's all over.

Before I could even respond the line went dead.

It was 3:00am. I sat in bed and cried harder than I had ever cried in my life.

God! How could you invite me into this nightmare? If you have the power to change this situation, WHY THE HELL won't you do it?!
I felt so out of control, the tears just wouldn't stop.

I physically felt ill, trying to calm my heart from pounding out of my chest. I began telling myself it was time to grieve. My body began to tighten up, and I felt nothing. Absolutely nothing. I had cried out every emotion and was left empty and numb.

I began thinking about how I would tell our family and friends our adoption process was over. She was gone. Jayda was never coming home.

All of a sudden, the phone rang, piercing my ears as the sound of the ring shot through the dark. I grabbed the phone, answered, and heard Jason screaming on the other end. His cry was unlike anything I'd ever heard come from him before.

ERICA! We got it! WE GOT IT! The order. We got the adoption order. She is OURS!

Wait. What?

I asked him to tell me exactly what was going on. What happened next put the breath back inside me in one giant gust.

He told me that just as they were waiting to begin the court hearing, a clerk walked in and told him that they were moving courtrooms. He was sent to the chambers of a different judge. The man sitting behind the desk said little to nothing as he focused on a stack of paperwork in front of him. A few minutes passed and Jason asked him what he was doing.

What am I doing? I'm writing your adoption order. I wish

someone would have adopted me when I was young. Now take your daughter home.

And that was it. It was one. The judge was the last key that finally opened the door. Just like that.

The most amazing part of this story is that the judge who granted our order never heard another adoption case after ours. It was his last day on the bench. The next day he moved to the Supreme Court.

The violent storm had passed. The calm after the storm was so sudden and encompassing, it almost felt as though everything we had endured had never happened.

Before I knew it, Jason was on his way home with our daughter. Everyone who knew us and the situation was in complete shock. No one could believe it actually happened. Honestly, neither could I. I was so used to the struggle by this point I didn't know how to function outside of it.

Jason was detained four times before getting clearance to leave the country. Jayda screamed most of the way home, and by the time he landed in Nashville and stepped off that plane he was in tears and literally kissed the ground. I was kissing Jason and Jayda and was memorizing the intricacies of the moment. I knew that this moment, this feeling, would somehow impact the rest of my life. I knew that we had come full circle. We had been invited to take a front row seat and wrap our brains around the orphan crisis.

Then God invited us to step into the ring. We fought till we were bruised and bleeding, and then she came home.

We had won.

The next three years we hid. We hid from the journey we'd been through. We settled into life with our new normal.

Jayda was a difficult child in the beginning. She had obsessions with food that controlled her behaviors. She was a fighter with a stubborn streak that I truly thought would tear the house down. She was like an earthquake that left nothing standing in her wake. I loved her so much yet at the same time felt like I couldn't love her enough to fix all the broken places in her heart. She pushed me to my limits, and I found myself sitting on the other side of her bedroom door in the aftermath, recovering from a battle of the wills, crying my eyes out, almost wishing she could go back. Not because I didn't love her, not because I had changed my mind. I just felt I wasn't enough to carry her heart and keep my own intact. It was so selfish. Yet that was my reality. I was in way over my head.

Slowly her raging storms grew quiet and less intense.

She eventually made it through a school day without causing controversy and finally started understanding how her family unit was supposed to work. At the end of the first year, we managed to finally make it out of the woods. We all survived, and this beautiful, fierce child began to blossom. I was reminded our lives had been carefully woven together, and now it was time to watch her become all she was destined to become. I knew there was something special about Jayda the moment I laid eyes on her. I knew that she would become someone, and her story would stand for something more than I could even begin to wrap my head around. I just didn't know what yet.

As Jayda got older and life settled, I couldn't help thinking about the mother who walked away. So selfless, I thought. Yet so selfish at the same time. How could she leave this child, this beautiful creation? How could she just walk away? She could have asked for help. She could have talked to relatives and asked someone in the family to raise her. How could she just walk away and never look back? On the other hand, was that the greatest gift she had ever given her daughter — a chance, a way out? Was turning her back the only way to live with the decision? I wondered what she was doing now, where was she living. How were her other children? Was she even still alive?

I felt like I owed Jayda's birthmother something. Actually — I felt like I owed her everything. Her darkest moment was my greatest joy. What a travesty that was. I had to somehow make it all right. I knew I had to find her. I had to go back. I had to find this mother, and I had to make it right.

I told Jason I was struggling with what we left behind in Sierra Leone. How could we ignore what we had seen when we had a daily reminder growing up under our roof? The heartbeat of Sierra Leone was front and center in our lives, and it was time we recognized that Jayda's presence wasn't just a reminder but another invitation to get our hands dirty once again. Another chance to do the next right thing.

Over the years, we made sure to stay in contact with Osseh, our driver in Freetown. We reached out and asked him to do some digging on Jayda's birthmother. We had hoped he could find out how she was doing. Find out if there was a way we could help support her.

A few weeks went by and eventually we heard from Osseh. He had found her. Still living in a camp, it seemed their family home was in disarray from the war and they had no means to repair it. We immediately went into fix-it mode. We pulled funds together that Christmas, and our family sent the money to Osseh to help rebuild Jayda's family home. Eventually the entire extended family moved back into it. Jayda's mother was safe, it seemed. She continued to have babies. That was hard for me to hear. Knowing that she was continually being used up and spit out, bringing lives into a world where they were not likely to survive. While Jayda's life was blossoming, her siblings were struggling.

♦ ♦ ♦

With a team of friends and family, Jason and I traveled back to Sierra Leone in December 2008. It had been four years since Jayda came home, and we had decided we would spend our time focusing on efforts to prevent the orphan statistic from growing in Sierra Leone. We would raise money here and there and focus on rebuilding homes and raising school scholarships for children. This would alleviate strain on families and hopefully we could prevent some families from abandoning their children because of poverty. It seemed like such a great idea at the time. I had no idea how quickly all that would change. I soon realized what it meant to live inside a life that was not my own and to realize it never really was in the first place. Discovering humanity, choosing to enter in and to be a part of it.

The trip back was everything we had hoped it would be. We made the long trek to the area of the country where Jayda's family home had been rebuilt. We were able to stop in and visit her relatives, take photographs, and spend time with the children living in the village. We met Jayda's grandmother for the very first time. It was so surreal to see her eyes, her features on the faces of her siblings and cousins. We delivered scholarships to close to 50 children at a school on the east side of town. Surprising the families was one of my most memorable moments. The joy that filled the children's faces and watching them jump up and down with excitement was almost too much for my heart.

After we left the school that day, Osseh mentioned there was an orphanage nearby. He thought it would be a good idea to stop in and see if we could offer any assistance. Honestly, I was tapped out. Our team was so exhausted, including my sister who was 7½ months pregnant. It seemed foolish to continue stretching ourselves, and I insisted we return to the hotel. Osseh wouldn't listen. He was dead set on visiting this center and promised it would only take a minute. That one decision changed the trajectory of our life.

Forever.

It also introduced me to the most beautiful baby in the entire world.

My Adama.

13.

THE COMPOUND
2009

Her eyes are homes of silent prayers.
—Alfred Lord Tennyson, In Memoriam, A.H.H., XXXII

Leaving Adama's grave that day felt eerily similar to how I felt leaving Jayda behind so many years before. It had been almost seven years to the day. The difference was that Jayda came home eventually. This goodbye to Adama was final. This goodbye would make itself at home and stay, never ending.

As we drove back to the guest house I began making

plans in my mind about the gravesite. I couldn't stand the thought of Adama staying buried as she was. It didn't feel right. She needed a stone. She needed a permanent resting place. Osseh felt that I needed to speak to Ina, the woman who had been taking care of Adama. He felt if I didn't involve her and she and her staff ever found out, it could cause a firestorm for us. I cringed at the thought. I can honestly say I have never despised someone more than I despised Ina. Did I hate her? Probably. Yes. Yes, I did. Just thinking about her made my skin crawl, and it also took me back to the first day we ever met.

I can remember the steep drive up to the compound. Billows of red dirt surrounded the car like smoke as we climbed the hill. Sweat was pouring down our backs, and weariness settled into our hearts. The team was so tired that day. But we didn't dare complain. At least we had water in our backpacks, a novelty in Sierra Leone during the dry season.

I began listening for children playing as we approached the gate. It was strange. Unlike other orphanages, this center was very quiet, in an odd something-isn't-quite-right kind of way.

The gate swung wide and we pulled into the drive. Slowly we watched staff emerge from the building and a few kids were scattered here and there. It was clear the children were trying to avoid us at first. We climbed out of the van and began to greet anyone who would say hello. I kneeled down in front of a small boy, maybe seven or eight years old, and reached out my hand for his.

Hi there, sweet one. It's nice to meet you.

I smiled and cautiously he smiled back. Then he grabbed my hand and began to show me around. News must have spread quickly because within moments children began coming out of the woodwork. I wasn't sure how many children were there but it felt like at least 100. I found it so odd that they were so quiet with so many inside the gates. I also noticed that the kids were a bit lethargic in nature and very, very small. Swollen bellies outnumbered the healthy ones. The record number of hollowed eyes and expressions took my breath right from my chest. The little boy whose hand I was still holding started walking me over to an area where a few babies were being held by other children. It felt like he assumed I was only there to hold babies. It broke my heart that he felt holding his hand wasn't enough for me. I tried to encourage him that I didn't need to see the babies. He insisted, and I fell under the pressure as he pushed me from behind. As we were making our way across the compound a young teenage girl approached. She carefully leaned in and quietly whispered into my ear.

Food?

She tugged gently on my backpack, assuming I had snacks inside and hoping I would share. I looked into her eyes and she began putting her hand to her mouth as if to beg.

I reached inside the bag and pulled out a pack of crackers. I handed her one and asked her when she had eaten last. She told me it had been four days. She tore into the food. As she ate, I studied her. Her hair was patchy and missing in places. Her clothes were no better than rags. She had no shoes. Her legs were covered in boils.

I don't really know how to explain what it does to a person to come face to face with a hungry and broken child. It all began to make sense in my mind. The children were quiet and lethargic because their bodies were breaking down from malnutrition. I had read about it. I knew what it looked like. I had seen it in the streets while driving through town. But I hadn't seen it up close and personal.

I grabbed the arm of a girl on our team and whispered,

Something is wrong here. Very wrong. Tell the team to take a hard look around and find out if there is food stored anywhere. Make note of the condition of the children, and look for anyone who stands out who we may need to help.

We swept the compound and began asking lots of questions. What we discovered was a gruesome facility that felt like an underground torture chamber.

The staff continued to plead with us, telling us that the children were in this kind of shape because there were no funds to care for them. In all my western naivety, I believed them.

Children who were so malnourished their breathing was labored, and their bodies shuddered with every breath. The storehouse where the rice should have been was empty. There was no water. The plumbing was broken so they had makeshift bathrooms for the children outside. Tarps held up by sticks. And instead of using their food bowls for rice, they used them to shit in. Shit was all over the ground. The smell was enough to knock you off your feet.

As we continued to explore the facility, staff led us to an outdoor area where a few children were laying on mats in the hot sun. At first look we could see they were special needs kids. One little girl was sitting up but unable to speak or use her hands. Her limbs were curled up and she had trouble making eye contact with anyone. They told us she was "demon possessed" and they were afraid to touch her. So, when they fed her or gave her any water to drink, they would toss it in her direction, and it would be up to her to get her hands on it. Obviously, she couldn't. She was literally starving to death while the rest of the center sat by and watched.

There was a little boy on a mat nearby. He looked to be about eight or nine months old, but we were told he was much closer to two years old. They also claimed he was special needs. He was able to sit up at times but he mostly lied on his side, making intense sucking noises with his mouth. We later discovered those noises were signs that he was in the last stage of starvation. This little boy had about two weeks to live. Then he would be gone. He was so severely malnourished his backbone would bend up through his stomach when you held him. It was absolutely horrifying.

A few moments later we were introduced to another baby.

Adama.

She was close to one year old, but looked to weigh only about seven or eight pounds. She was so malnourished her hair was patchy and orange, just like so many others in the compound. She screamed nonstop. Her cries tore into me like a freight train. In that moment I knew she had a piece of my heart I would never get back. Little did I know at the time that our journey together was just getting started.

After sweeping the place, we counted at least 30 kids so malnourished they needed immediate medical attention.

We had to do something. But what? How do you fix something like this? Where did we start?

As we were frantically trying to decide what to do and how to do it, I was thanking God under my breath that we had found this place. It was clear to me that this was the reason we were meant to come. Finding these children gave them a chance. We could fix this, right? What I didn't know was that there was another reason we fell upon this orphanage. A miracle was about to unfold before my eyes.

The woman running the place approached me, speaking very little English. I used the help of someone who could interpret, and she asked me the oddest question.

You are Iye's mom, am I right?

I'm sorry I am not sure I understand you. What did you say?

She asked again.

You are Iye Moses's mother, right?

I stood there shell-shocked. How on Earth did this woman know anything about me, my family, or my daughter? I had never seen this woman before. I had never met her. I was stunned, and, honestly, a bit scared. No one knew we had been to Sierra Leone in 2004 and had adopted a Sierra Leonian daughter. Very few knew her African name was "Iye."

I'm sorry, why are you asking me this?

Because I know your daughter. I found her in the refugee camp and left her at the orphanage years ago.

Wait. You are telling me you knew my daughter Iye and you found her in the camp?

Yes. She was a vulnerable child, and I rescued her. I also rescued her brother.

The anxiety began building in my chest as I tried to process the conversation.

Ohhhh! You must have the wrong child. My daughter doesn't have a brother.

Oh but she does *have a brother. When I dropped them at the orphanage they told me he was too old and made me take him away. He is still with me today. Would you like to meet him?*

I lost feeling in my legs and my stomach dropped. Could this be true? How on Earth could it be true? There are millions of people and thousands of refugees in this country. How could I have stumbled upon the *one* woman who was responsible for leaving my daughter in an orphanage and raising a brother we never knew existed?

Before I could even answer, she began shouting at someone in Krio.

Emmanuel! Emmanuel!

Over and over again.

I continued to focus on my breath, and did my best to

stay upright. I kept feeling like I might pass out. The heat and sweat combined with my heart racing and emotional distress was not a good combination.

From around the corner came a young man. He looked to be around 18 years old. I knew instantly she was telling the truth. He was the spitting image of Jayda. As soon as he saw me, he lit up like a Christmas tree and came running. The embrace between us was a jolt to my system. I just could not believe this was happening. I stepped back and looked him in the eyes, smiling through my tears the best I could.

Thankfully he spoke excellent English.

Hi, Emmanuel. My name is Erica.

I know who you are, mom. I've been waiting all these years for you to come.

What? He *knew* about me? And he called me mom.

The next several days felt like an out-of-body experience. I learned the truth about Jayda's history. It was nothing like what we were told leading up to her adoption. Emmanuel and Jayda were brought to the orphanage and told at the door that he was "too old" and that no one would want him. So, they agreed to take Jayda and closed the door on Emmanuel. Hearing him recall the last time he saw her, the sting during the goodbye, the hopelessness he felt when leaving her behind. It was more than any child should have to endure.

What was I supposed to do with this? Jayda had a brother. A young man with no support system, living in and working for a woman running an orphanage. He made my heart bleed. I wasn't sure how to fix the injustice that he had been left behind. I had to make it right somehow. What was appropriate? What wasn't? What did the culture expect of me? What did I expect of myself? What did Emmanuel hope I could offer him?

14.

THE BENCH
2009

Do not stand idly by if you witness injustice. You must intervene. You must interfere. —Elie Wiesel, 2011 Commencement Address at Washington University

We spent the rest of that trip working out a plan to transport as many kids as possible to the local hospital. After doing our best to examine as many as we could, we knew there were at least 30 children with immediate medical needs. Several were literally starving to death. We had to act quickly. Unfortunately, we had hit the weekend, which meant it would be really hard to get anything accomplished.

We decided to load up the very sickest children first, and I took Adama. We hired a physician to visit the orphanage and examine the remaining children. I never imagined we would be turned away from a medical facility that day. We drove from one hospital to the next and were turned away over and over again. Why? Simply because it was Sunday.

These are the moments that will make you or break you in countries like Sierra Leone. There is so much opposition to help. It's sometimes next to impossible to get anyone to act swiftly or to move with intention — even when you have dying children on your hands. It blew my mind that hospitals would refuse to take in a child because it was a weekend. But they did it. And we couldn't do a thing about it.

Eventually we found a hospital willing to examine the kids. By this time it was late in the day, and the sun was starting to cast shadows down the hallways of the building. There was no electricity. There wasn't a single fan. No airflow. The halls were stagnant and dismal. We sat on a long wooden bench for hours as sweat poured down our backs. You would think in conditions like this the kids would have gotten restless, noisy, and difficult to manage. But it wasn't like that. The kids had to work so hard just to breathe in and out. Their little bodies were so frail. They sat in our arms like rag dolls. They only moved around when we would readjust, repositioning only when we did. We tried to keep them awake, tried to get them to smile and interact with us. Every so often you could see them. There behind the eyes were beautiful souls forced to endure pain no one ever should. I could feel Adama's bones protruding through her diaper, settling into my thighs. I began to memorize her tiny wrists and fingers wrapped around mine.

I had begged Osseh not to go to the center that day. We were so tired from the work at the school. What if he hadn't insisted? We never would have found these children. They would have died. We were placed in a position that forced us to intervene, but I didn't go looking for it. This made me wonder what it would be like if we did go looking. What might we find?

I continued studying Adama, watching her as she studied me. That's when it happened. That's when I knew I loved her.

She was so small. Sitting up on my lap, trying hard to keep her balance. Every time I said her name, she looked up at me, eyes wide with wonder. I am sure my white skin was strange to her. Each time I thought she might cry, I would sing ever so softly under my breath, rocking her back and forth. Her heart would stop racing, settling her a bit. She wouldn't stop staring at me. I couldn't stop staring at her either. It was as though we were the only two in the whole world, destined to find one another. Our worlds were meant to collide. I knew it. And somehow, as young as she was, I think she knew it too.

After their examinations, one of the children was immediately admitted to the malnutrition unit. The physician was concerned we may be too late. He made no promises but said they would try everything they could to bring this little guy back to life. Kelly never left his side.

Within a matter of days, he was wide-eyed and alert. He was bearing weight on his legs and showing major signs of improvement. After about three weeks, the boy was discharged. He had gained a substantial amount of weight and was responding well to his nutritional regimen. They mentioned to us that it would take some time to determine just how significantly his brain had been affected due to the malnutrition. He would likely experience significant delays as he grew up. Regardless — his recovery really was a miracle. He was alive and strong enough to leave the hospital. The team desperately needed that glimmer of hope. We knew we had so much work ahead of us in the fight to protect all the children we had met in that place. Down the road, that little boy beat more odds than I can count. He was eventually adopted by a family in the United States.

The team spent our last few days in-country gathering as many supplies as we could. We loaded multiple trucks with bags of rice and water and delivered them to the orphanage before we left. According to our calculations, we left plenty of food and supplies to get everyone at the orphanage through the next few months. As soon as we got back to the States, we planned to begin a fundraising initiative that would support the center moving forward.

If only it had been that easy.

Raising funds is never easy. Jason and I spent so much time away from home, sharing the story of what we uncovered with anyone who would listen. We spoke to churches and Sunday school classes. We shared in living rooms and in schools. Slowly but surely, people began to step into the trenches with us. Word began to spread and funds began to creep in. Within weeks we had started raising enough money to make a difference in the staff's ability to feed and house the children. We started sending regular monthly support. Osseh would take that money, purchase supplies, and deliver them each month. We felt like we were finally making a difference where it counted.

In the meantime, I couldn't stop thinking about Adama. Jason and I didn't take long to make the decision to adopt her. We knew she was meant to be ours. Our fight for Jayda had taught us that the road may not be easy, but Adama was worth it. Whatever the journey held for us, we were in 100%. We contacted the woman running the center and shared with her our desire to adopt Adama. She seemed ecstatic. She said she would do whatever was necessary to help with the process. We hired an attorney, the best in the city at the time, and we were told the process would likely move very quickly. It seemed we were golden.

We announced our plans to our family, began decorating a nursery, doing all the things you do when you are stepping into the world of adoption.

Then one day, I got a phone call.

I could hear Osseh on the other end of the line and I could tell he was very upset. He began telling me how he had started doing random check-ins at the orphanage. The rice and water was running out at an alarming rate. He did some digging and found out the people running the facility were taking the supplies we sent and selling them on the streets for cash. The kids were still not being fed or taken care of. I couldn't believe it. The more we dug into the situation, the more we realized we were in bed with an exploitation ring. That was the bottom line. The people running the place were keeping the children underfed and malnourished on purpose. Their plan was to exploit them, showing off their plight to westerners like us, in hopes that they could collect money. Not to help the children — to pad their pockets.

Jason and I were reeling. As we kept unpacking it and wrapping our brains around it, everything started to make sense. It explained why the children were so leery of us, why they hid and were so afraid to engage.

I didn't sleep for days. I had no idea what to do with the information we had been given. Obviously, we could no longer send support. But how would we help the children? How would we rescue them from this horrific place?

My brain went into overdrive. My answer to the problem was so simple in my head.

WE OPEN OUR OWN ORPHANAGE.

We contact the police and report the abuse. The government will step in, remove the children, and place them with us. Easy.

Sounds crazy, I know.

It was.

15.

RIGHTING THE WRONG
2009

*There comes a time when one must take a position
that is neither safe, nor politic, nor popular,
but he must also take it because
his conscience tells him it is right.*
—Martin Luther King, Jr., *I Have a Dream*

I know so many people thought we had lost our minds when we decided to launch our own care center. There were many heartfelt discussions. There were many concerns voiced. While I listened, I knew — and those trying to talk sense into us knew — nothing was going to stop us.

Sometimes I wish I had given a little more thought to the fact that a center was a 24/7 facility. It wasn't like a well project where you raise money, go into a community, break down the soil, dig a well, and then celebrate the water flowing from the ground. And you move on. Mission accomplished. Opening an orphanage was no small undertaking. This was a decision that would alter the course of our entire lives forever.

I didn't really think about that at the time. Honestly, I was in "band-aid" mode. I was thinking that with one swift sweep of my super hero cape I could change it all for the children we found. I never thought about the damage I would cause or the pain that would come down the road. Granted, a band-aid is better than bleeding out, but I know now the biggest contribution I could have ever made to a society exploiting children was not to open an orphanage, but rather to expose the injustice on a grand scale that would bring change. But instead of moving with precision and planning, I let my heart call the shots. I wore my rose-colored glasses and jumped headfirst into the deep.

For several months we raised funds. We found ourselves visiting the same people who joined in on the cause from day one. We spent time updating them on the crisis at hand and filling them in on our decision to take matters into our own hands. Living room by living room, church by church, family by family, the impossible began to seem like a glass ceiling we could break through if we really wanted to. I think by the time we boarded the plane in September 2009, we had collected at least $50,000. That seemed like more than enough at the time. I laugh when I think back on that. I had a spreadsheet with our budget. We would lease a building for a year, hire staff, stock the place with supplies, and BOOM! We would be in business. Once the orphanage was up and running, the plan was to return to the States and pursue child sponsorship to support the cause. Sounded good, seemed to make sense, but I clearly had lost my mind. It didn't happen that way. Thankfully, I've come to see now that a willing heart can do a lot of good. We did make significant headway, but we also stepped into a warzone. One we are still fighting in ten years later.

***

I traveled with a handful of amazing women. I carefully chose those who came along, making sure they could handle the hard work ahead. They were from all different walks of life, all carrying talents and abilities we needed on the ground. But most importantly they all came with bleeding hearts and open arms. Together we would do the unthinkable. There was no other option. We were in Sierra Leone for ten days, so we would launch a center in the time we had. While many of the women cleaned, furnished, and prepared the building, several others went downtown to purchase supplies and stock the storehouse. Some women spent their days interviewing potential staff and deciding who would land the handful of jobs we had available. And last but not least — we still had to get the kids released to us.

My own plans were also coming together. I had decided it made all the sense in the world to set our court date for Adama's adoption while I was on the ground launching the center. My mother-in-law traveled with me and planned to act as my nanny while I worked during the day. The thought of staying in the guest house and getting to know Adama made her heart explode. She was so excited, ready to meet this beautiful little baby I had told her so much about.

My attorney had told me that the adoption would process quickly so I was prepared to also bring Adama home with us if all things worked out as planned. I had a suitcase just for her. It was filled with diapers, clothing, toys, snacks, and paperwork. Loads and loads of paperwork.

Before moving into full swing, the team and I decided it was important to get to Ina's as quickly as possible. We needed to assess the current situation inside the walls, and I was dying to get my hands on my little girl. Our hope was that, woman to woman, we could get Ina alone and talk sense into her. I felt like maybe she was being coerced into the way she was operating. I couldn't imagine she was behind it all. I thought that helping her see what she was doing to the kids, and offering her a job, would convince her to release the kids to us. Because I wasn't sure who had alliances to Ina or where the tribal ties connected, I knew reporting her to the government was risky. So, if there was an easier way, we were set on finding it.

I felt like my heart was about to burst as we pulled into the drive of Ina's center. It had been eight months since we found this place, and so much had happened in that short time. Knowing that we were on course to rescue these kids, and knowing my daughter was inside those walls, made my stomach turn in knots. I was ready yet I was questioning myself all along the way. Was I capable of pulling something like this off? I felt like I was walking blind. Honestly, I was.

As we got out of the vehicles, I don't know what I really expected to find. Osseh had warned me it wasn't good. We purposefully showed up unannounced. We didn't want the staff cleaning up or hiding anything. We wanted to see what was happening inside that gate when no one was around.

As we made our way through the center, I knew that Ina wouldn't cave as easily as we thought. As soon as I approached her, I could sense something had changed. She seemed guarded, a bit aloof, and not very interested in greeting me. I am sure she wasn't happy about the unexpected visit. She handed Adama to me, but I could tell she didn't really want to.

We had a photographer on our team, and she began documenting everything we saw there. She was great at shooting without anyone realizing it. She grabbed photos of the bulging bellies and video capturing the cries of neglected children. She took pictures of the makeshift bathrooms, the feces filling the compound. We had a record now of the empty storehouse, the broken well, and she even stumbled across a room that had probably 40 children locked inside. We still don't know why they were being held there. The center was as horrific as the last time we saw it. Only this time we were well aware it was not because of poverty that these children were suffering — it was because of evil. We think death is the worst atrocity in cases like this, that grief is the hardest cross to bear. But I'm learning after 14 years in Sierra Leone, there are worse things than death. Much worse.

Anger swallowed us whole that day. It took my entire team captive. We knew our plans for the trip were about to change. We could all feel the battle ahead.

We left the center that day determined to expose the injustice inside the gate. If we had to, we would also expose the people behind it. We wanted to make sure we didn't make a move that would further hurt the children, but we also had to balance our silence. We could not stand on the side of the oppressor. We had to stand for truth.

The next day I decided to try to kill two birds with one stone. While meeting with the ministry about our adoption, I would also take that opportunity to tell them what we had found at Ina's place. We were in the middle of registering our organization with the government. They knew we had plans to open a center. So, in my mind, I assumed once they saw what we had discovered they would agree to move the kids. Adama would be in my custody finally, and the children would all be safe.

So off we went, bound and determined to do the right thing.

16.

RUN CHILD RUN
2009

Hell is empty, and all the devils are here.
—William Shakespeare, *The Tempest*

We got to the Ministry of Social Welfare armed and ready for battle. Our computers were filled with photographs and accounts of what we had witnessed in the center. We also had proof of the financial support we had been sending and proof it had been mismanaged. We had documentation showing this group of people was running an exploitation ring, keeping children in harm's way, and taking advantage of donations meant for the kids.

Erica Stone

We sat down in the office of the minister with hearts beating out of our chests.

When the minister arrived, he seemed surprised to see so many of us in his office. I brought along a few of the team members, knowing it would take all of us to communicate this story correctly. I didn't want to leave anything out, and I knew having multiple people supporting the claims we were making, multiple people as witnesses, would help our case. If the minister knew so many of us were aware of the atrocities, he may be more inclined to act on behalf of the children. As soon as we made it past the pleasantries, he asked why we were there, and we moved into action.

Over the next hour or so we shared everything we had witnessed over the last several months. We pulled our chairs right up to his desk, all peering over the computer, leaning in and pointing out every atrocity. One by one by one. We told him about our first visit, about the monthly support. We shared about the discovery of missing food. We showed him the photographs of the children. Each picture was more gripping than the last. We showed him the horrible living conditions we had documented. He became more and more uncomfortable. Shaking his head, muttering under his breath. He seemed moved by the information and almost as equally disturbed as we were.

We told him about the orphanage we had just started.

We shared with him we had a full team on the ground engaged in the launch of the center, and that we were ready to take in children. All we needed was his office to grant us our registration. We pleaded with him to allow us the chance to serve the children we had been trying to support for so many months. We begged him to allow us to rescue these kids.

He made a lot of promises that day. He promised to "look into it." He promised to make sure the hellhole we showed him would be "shut down." He promised that nothing like this would be tolerated under his watch. It had seemed so easy. I actually felt myself leaning into this man, counting on him.

Eventually we had the chance to talk about my adoption for a few moments. I shared with him that my daughter was in that terrible place and that I needed to get her out. I let him know that the woman running the center had stopped taking my calls. I shared that I desperately needed him to intervene on my behalf.

Then he asked me who I was dealing with. He wanted to know who was calling the shots.

As soon as I told him her name, something changed in his face. It was in that moment the battle shifted. I couldn't quite put my finger on it at the time, but, with the mention of Ina's name, his face told me something changed. I could feel with certainty our position was threatened. In that moment, tribal ties trumped justice as is so often the case in countries like Sierra Leone where connections between groups of people belie all reasoning.

The team left hopeful. I left concerned. An eerie, dark cloud enveloped me. It felt almost evil in nature. But I didn't speak of it. I wouldn't dare. Maybe I was wrong. God, I hoped I was wrong, but something didn't feel right.

The minister granted us permission to remove the children. We planned to return the next day with a support unit to accompany us to the orphanage to retrieve the kids. The entire way back to the hotel, the car was filled with anxious chatter about what the coming days would hold.

In the meantime, most of the team was at the hotel spread out between two rooms, enjoying the air conditioning after a very hot, exhausting day. Some of us were planning agendas, some of us were showering, and several were sleeping. It felt like the day was giving us a moment to breathe before all hell broke loose.

We took shelter in that quiet; we loved it actually. I felt like we could all finally think. I replayed the conversation at the ministry over and over again in my mind. I so badly wanted the minister to be a good man, with solid intentions. Someone who didn't stand on the side of the oppressors, caving to political corruption, but rather a political giant who would choose to free children instead of enslaving them.

As I was chatting with a few girls in one room, we heard a commotion outside. I stepped out to see what was happening and couldn't believe my eyes.

A teenage boy who had been living in the hellhole had made his way to our hotel looking for us. I don't know how he escaped, or why, but I knew it was a purposeful visit. If you only knew how far he had traveled to get to where we were.

He was a bit unsteady. His voice shook. He started asking for my cousin Lori who had traveled with us. He mentioned her name over and over again, demanding to see her. It was clear he didn't want to talk to us. He only wanted to see Lori. I ran as fast as I could and threw open the hotel room door, yelling for her. I can remember how she jumped out of bed like the place was on fire. I suppose I was yelling like the place was, in fact, going up in smoke. Her eyes were wide. She didn't ask any questions. She just followed me. I'm not sure if I made any sense, but I told her as much as I could get out. I told her Sam had run away from the orphanage. He had traveled all the way to the hotel and was demanding to see her. Lori cried.

She brought Sam back to our hotel room and the child began to pour out his heart. He emptied every crevice of his heart and soul, sharing details of a life I couldn't even begin to imagine. He told us he had run away to find us, knowing that we would help them. He thought we were the children's only hope. Many of the kids knew he had run and helped aid in his escape. He told us we had to get his siblings out. He couldn't leave them behind. We knew if we sent him back, he could face a severe punishment by those running the place. But we also knew if he stayed with us, it could be worse for him. We were at a loss. We didn't know what exactly to do, but we knew that we could not stop fighting for the kids. We had to do whatever it took to get them out.

We decided we needed someone else to corroborate Sam's story. Not because we didn't believe him, but we knew if we could get at least one more person willing to admit they had witnessed the same abuse, it would only strengthen Sam's testimony. So, Osseh made contact with Emmanuel. We sent word and requested for him to come to the hotel. When he showed up and saw Sam there, he didn't seem surprised. It was like he knew this was all going to happen.

Emmanuel sat down and verified everything Sam told us. It was horrifying. They recalled abuse so wretched we had team members get up and leave the room. Stories that painted pictures of children being treated like animals. One story I'll never forget. They talked about the staff placing a bowl of rice in the middle of the room. They would choose two children to meet in the middle and would force them to fight for it. They would also make the rest of the children watch. Whoever was left standing was allowed to eat that night.

They kept all bathrooms locked and forced children to use their food bowls to urinate and defecate in. We had seen this when we were there and also had photographs to prove it. This testimony only further solidified what we knew was going on.

After hours of talking, we encouraged the boys to shower, helped them into clean clothes, and fed them.

I knew that the hardest part was still to come. We needed these boys to go to social welfare and report the abuse they had endured. I knew it would be a tall order, a request they shouldn't even have to consider. Knowing that our position with the ministry was shaky, and still not sure why, I had to get these boys to talk in front of the people who mattered.

I'll never forget the pride they portrayed when we finally got the nerve up to ask them to go with us to social welfare. They never hesitated. Sam and Emmanuel were true warriors. They had no intention of sitting silent. It was their mission to raise the alarm. They told us their hearts told them to run and to fight. They would not back down. They wouldn't stop until they rescued their friends. Arm in arm, we took the next step. We sounded an alarm that would eventually backfire on us.

When we arrived the next day, the minister acted very preoccupied. His coldness sent chills down my spine. He casually began to make excuses for why he could not support the transfer of the children to us, blaming it on red tape and how it could be perceived. We introduced him to the boys and had each of them give their testimony, hoping he would recognize he had a duty to these kids.

It didn't work. He asked to speak to me alone.

As everyone made their way out of the office, my fears began to take shape.

He told me that after careful consideration he could not give me an approval to proceed to court for my adoption, nor could he give me custody of Adama. He blamed it again on red tape and public perception. With the trafficking scandal in the papers, granting an adoption to a white woman opening an orphanage would seem conspicuous to all watching. He acted as though he was trying to protect me, saying the last thing he would want is for me to be seen as a trafficker in his country. He told me I would have to make a choice. He would do one thing or the other for me.

Option One: He would grant the registration and allow us to open the center, *but* I had to abandon my adoption petition.

Option Two: He would grant the approval to adopt Adama, *but* I would have to abandon the opening of the orphanage.

I could do one or the other. Not both.

Either decision would come with a significant cost.

Either way, my back was against the wall. Either way, I wouldn't, *couldn't* make the right choice.

17.

THE CHOICE
2009

*You see, I had always intended to keep you.
Which made all the difference in the way our
hearts broke upon saying goodbye.*
—Tiffany Aurora, *The Wild Keeps Her Holy*

I don't really know how to express in words what it felt like leaving the ministry that day. I want to paint the story for you in words that would give you insight, something that would explain what was happening in my brain. But, the fact is that I was in denial. Nothing I felt or believed in those days following the ultimatum was true. That makes it hard to be honest with you. It's hard to explain exactly what I was going through when I feel so ashamed by it.

I'd like to be able to say that I chose my daughter that day. Like all good mothers would. I'd like to say I sacrificed it all for her.

But I can't.

On the other side of the ultimatum, I wish I could say that I chose the greater good with a full heart and a fire in my bones urging me forward with purpose. That I sacrificed one to save many. That sounds so brave and heroic. Doesn't it?

But I can't.

I didn't wear a single shade of anything valiant. My superhero cape was gone. I only made matters worse on every side. Children were hanging in the balance, and every step I took only seemed to make it worse. I found myself in a position I never expected to be in, one I wasn't prepared for.

Instead of thinking about Adama and the others sitting under the weight of my decision, I was thinking about myself. If I chose Adama, how would I explain that decision to those waiting on me back at the hotel? I couldn't abandon opening the orphanage. What would everyone think of me? So many people had given money to get it up and running. What about those on the ground pouring themselves into the launch? There was no way I could stop that moving train. They would hate me. I would appear weak and selfish. We had already promised jobs to countless people in Sierra Leone. What would we tell them if we shut down the whole operation?

And what about Adama? I knew better than anyone that if I kept pushing for Adama's release things would get ugly. She was already being used as a pawn. The center had stopped answering my calls. Whether I went after her, or advocated for all of the kids, either way, it would end badly. I knew if I continued fighting for those kids to be released, they would find a way to keep Adama from me just to be spiteful.

I knew in my heart, this was the beginning of a goodbye. But I told myself a story. One with a perfect little ending. It went something like this.

I would abandon my adoption petition. We would launch our orphanage and continue advocating to take as many kids from Ina's as we could. I would wait three to six months, let the drama settle down, and then quietly come back into the country and re-file my petition. I would hire someone to keep eyes on Adama, to make sure she was being cared for while we waited for the perfect time to make our move. She would be okay. I would survive. I would go back every few months and visit, making sure my time in-country was used to strengthen my adoption case once it went to court. This way everything stayed in play. We could go home telling all of our donors we had successfully launched our center. I would also get what I wanted — my daughter — eventually. I told myself the government officials could be trusted. I told myself the minister had my back. I told myself Ina would eventually turn Adama over to me. When Ina's money ran out and she could no longer care for Adama, she would release her. She loved Adama after all. She wouldn't let her waste away under her watch. There had to be a heart somewhere inside that woman. I would find it. I would win her over. It would only be a matter of time.

And I believed it all.

Every single lie.

Every lie I told myself settled into my heart as something that was true. Even though I knew deep down it wasn't true. None of it was true. I knew opening the center was a risk that could cost me everything. But I didn't feel I could walk in freedom outside of it. I never felt free to make a choice *for* Adama. I wasn't free to love her the way I wanted to. I had obligations — so many obligations — that came first. I reasoned it all away in my mind. I chose to take on the persona and title of orphanage founder and advocate for justice. But really, I was a mother who chose her "job" over her child. I put Adama second. She paid for it with her life. I painted a picture of a group of women saving the world, rescuing kids and changing lives. Meanwhile, Adama was on her way to her grave, and I sat by letting it all happen. All because I cared so much about what other people would think.

I spent so many years worrying about what people

thought of me. Other people's opinions of me ruled my existence and validated my decisions. I wished that for once, just once, I'd listened to my gut and the one voice begging me to find another way. But that voice was snuffed out.

Until now.

When I got back to the hotel, I was honest with the team. I told them all what had happened with the minister. I told them I was given a chance to decide and knew there really was no choice. We had to go through with the opening of the center. The concern on their faces told me that they knew what I knew. They were well aware this decision could cost me my daughter. But I did my best to convince them I would be back in a few months and would finish up her adoption. I made sure to speak with as much confidence as I could. I ensured everyone that I was okay and that we had to focus on the task at hand. Continuing to sound the alarm, someone somewhere at some point would listen. We would not stop until those children were safe inside our walls.

As we wrapped up the talk, I noticed my mother-in-law slip away to the bathroom. After what seemed like an eternity, she came out with tears streaming down her face. All she had wanted was to bring her granddaughter home. It wasn't easy for her to travel across the world at her age, and she had been sick most of the time she had been there. She was a trooper, working herself to death while she waited for Adama to be given to us. Now that the reality hit her — Adama wasn't coming home — she broke into a million pieces.

We continued working for the next few weeks and finally opened the center, complete with a healthy food supply and full-time staff. We also took in several children. We staged several more sit-ins with other government agencies. It did nothing. In the meantime, word had spread through the city that there was a war of sorts between a Sierra Leonian and a group of white women. The word on the street was that we were "stealing" children from her. That was not good. "Stealing" eventually turned into "child trafficking." We didn't think too much of it but decided it was in our best interest to hire extra security for our hotel, just in case a riot broke out with us at the center of the controversy. It was a bit unnerving when that security company arrived. The man we hired showed up with a very large gun and stood watch on our steps from that day on.

After lots of moving around the city we finally found someone who seemed willing to help us and the kids. He was a community leader near Ina's center, far on the east side of town. He was also a prominent member of the city council. We heard the city council might have jurisdiction that trumped social welfare. He came to our hotel where we told him everything. He felt we had a strong case and immediately moved into action. He picked up his phone and called for an emergency city council meeting. He told us to be at the city council's office the next morning with all our documentation and to also bring any other people along who could testify to the atrocities we had witnessed.

That night none of us could sleep. We were amped. We thought we had finally found our knight in shining armor.

The next day was a whirlwind. After hours of deliberation, the council voted to send a squad of vehicles to intervene and remove the children from Ina's. We couldn't believe it. Finally someone was listening. I can remember the feeling in my stomach as the rescue squad packed up and drove out of the parking lot. The councilman was all smiles, chanting as he left, yelling out the window that good would prevail. We raced back to the center to prepare for the children's arrival.

Hours went by. No word.

I remember all of us sitting in a circle together, in an empty building, praying and quietly crying.

Finally, late in the day, we got the call I will never forget.

The councilman had made every attempt to remove the kids, but the rescue caused such a commotion he felt it was dangerous to proceed. Chaos and rioting broke out, causing the rescue squad to abandon the mission altogether.

We were devastated. If I could only explain what it sounded like. The wails and cries of the team and staff who had prayerfully waited for the children to arrive. To this day, I don't know exactly what kind of power Ina holds over the city. I know her tribal ties are strong, and I know almost everyone is afraid of her. And because of that, she won the battle.

But the war — the one we are still fighting today — she will not win.

18.

HOTEL 510
2009

We are endurance.
We are steadfast bravery. We are not moving.
—Tyler Knott Gregson, *Daily Haiku on Love*

As news — gossip, really — of the failed rescue mission continued to spread through the city, things became unsafe for many of our staff living on the east side of Freetown. Riots had broken out, and one of our caregivers was arrested after trying to make her way through town. I suppose people had gotten word she worked for us and they accused her of trafficking. An altercation broke out between her and those working for Ina, and she was thrown in jail. Not good, considering she was pregnant with twins. I could also see the uneasiness spreading through the team. They had all been such troopers, but let's be real. They said yes to a mission trip to open a center, not a justice mission.

The day before the team left, we got a call from the U.S. Embassy. When I looked down at my ringing phone, I didn't recognize the number. I was a bit nervous about answering. I had no idea who was looking for me or trying to get in touch with me. I was scared.

The woman on the other end told me her name and that she was calling from the U.S. Embassy. She very frankly said,

It seems there is a riot that has broken out on the east side of town. The information we are getting is that it is due to your work in the country. There are allegations of trafficking. It is likely if you are found by the police you will be arrested. I would suggest contacting your families. While we cannot keep you from arrest, we can visit you should you be placed into custody and advocate for your fair and dignified treatment. Here is my cell if you run into any trouble. Oh — and — good luck.

She ended the call before I could really say anything or ask her any questions. I was stunned. Shell-shocked. I looked around the room at the other girls and, as calmly as possible, told them what the call was about. They all handled it better than I expected. There were no tears. No one was freaking out. They all calmly called their families. I was not thrilled about calling mine. I knew Jason would lose his ever-loving mind. Rather than make the call, I decided to do what I do under stress: deflect and shelf the inevitable. I pulled out my make-up bag and started applying a fresh face. I still remember one of the girls looking at me in disbelief.

Um, Erica. Why are you putting on make-up right now? You should be calling Jason!

I simply said,

Well if I'm gonna get arrested, and my face ends up on Fox News, I need to look half-way decent!

The response broke through the stress in the room and we all erupted into laughter, the belly kind. We laughed so hard, we cried, and then the tears didn't stop.

The next day was hard. Really hard. I still remember looking around the room as the team began packing their things for their trip home. It felt like we had been there for ten years. At the same time, the trip had flown by. A few of us had decided to stay behind. We just could not leave without resolving the fight for custody of the children. We had to find a way to rescue those kids. But not all of the team could stay. These women left their families behind and now were caught up in something none of us ever saw coming. They had to go home.

As I watched them pack and repack, trying to squeeze

their belongings back into place for the long trip home, I felt such sadness creep into my bones. A wave of thankfulness overwhelmed me in the same way. We would have never made it this far without them. It took every single one of us to get that center off the ground. It took every single one of them, their unique talents and personalities, their hearts and their souls, to create what we created in Sierra Leone in such a short time. I was scared to stay without them. Sad to see them go. I wanted to get on that plane, too. I wanted to run from the pain that was closing in around me. I watched my mother-in-law pack her things, putting Adama's diapers and toys back in her suitcase. Tears streaming down her face. The pain was fierce and always present. I just kept pushing it down.

But as they loaded into the vehicles to leave, I cried my eyes out. As they pulled out of the gate, I felt almost like we had been left stranded. What were we going to do now? Only three of us were left. How would we maneuver this situation? How would we get those kids out? And would we get home without being arrested?

That night, after the team left, Osseh got a phone call. Surprisingly, it was from the city councilman. He was calling on behalf of Ina and her people running the orphanage. He told Osseh that they were tired of the chaos, and they were ready to "negotiate." They asked us to meet them that night at Hotel 510.

When Osseh told us what they had said, I wasn't sure

how to respond. It was already late and dark out. The embassy was clear we needed to stay put and avoid East Freetown. Yet Osseh seemed to think going would be a good idea.

We didn't stop to think anymore about it. We jumped into Osseh's sport utility and the three of us crammed in the back. We were hoping we would be less conspicuous back there. Yeah right.

We began the long drive to the other side of the city. The traffic was horrible, as always, even late at night. We felt pretty secure thinking that most people would be going home by now and that maybe the riots had slowed a bit in intensity.

We were wrong.

As we came into an area called Kissee, the crowds seemed to grow. People were everywhere. We found ourselves shrinking into the seats trying not to be seen. When traffic and crowds grow, the congestion is unreal. People are literally holding onto cars as they cross streets. It would have been very easy for someone to see us in the back of the truck as they passed by.

Unfortunately, Osseh couldn't quite remember where Hotel 510 was. He had to stop to ask for directions. This was *not* good. People began peering into Osseh's truck. We were literally lying in the floorboards trying to hide from everyone outside.

We eventually found our way down a side ally and

turned into the parking area of Hotel 510. By this time, it was raining. We ran inside and found the front desk. The foyer of the hotel was dark. There was little lighting, and it was smoky and smelled like mildew and hookah smoke. The man at the desk didn't even wait for us to tell him who we were. He already knew. He simply pointed down the hall and said,

Room 3.

We nodded a polite thank you and proceeded down the hallway. When we came upon the door to Room 3, I began to feel very uneasy. The number on the door was hanging sideways, and the door was ajar. We could hear commotion inside the room.

I took a very deep breath and held it, pushing open the door and walking inside.

I honestly don't remember everything about the room. I was on a mission and was ready to confront the people holding my daughter. The other two girls on my team caught a little more of the picture and told me about it later.

We entered a small room with a queen bed, two chairs, a dresser with a small tube television, and a small pendant lamp hanging from the ceiling in the corner. There were beer bottles everywhere. In the room was the man who runs Ina's center and the city councilman. Both men were drunk. Our arrival startled them both. They tried to get up, but we motioned for them to stay seated. We carefully sat down on the bed.

Immediately Osseh and I began asking the men questions.

What did they want from us? Why did they call us here late in the night? Why this hotel? What were we there to negotiate?

They began chattering about things that didn't matter, circling the issue. I could feel my blood boiling. I was trying so hard to keep my poker face, to pretend like I didn't really care about the meeting. I wanted to appear stronger than them, but I was getting close to the ugly cry. I knew this man could turn over Adama if he wanted to. I knew he could end all of this. Just as I was about to start begging, my two teammates broke through the conversation and began yelling at the men to turn off the TV. They said they couldn't concentrate until they shut it down. That seemed strange to me so I glanced over at the TV and realized what all the commotion was about. Porn was center stage. Of course it was.

The men laughed. Our skin crawled with disgust. They unplugged the TV, and I got right down to it.

I'm gonna ask you one more time. What do you want from us?

Easy. Ten thousand dollars will give you a child. You can have as many as you want. Adama? $10,000. The others? Also, $10,000.

I almost collapsed.

Osseh became very angry. They all started arguing in Krio, and before I knew it Osseh was ushering us out. He was floored that the councilman had participated in this situation. It felt like things couldn't get any worse. As we made our way to the car in the pouring rain, we all began to laugh. Was this really happening? Did *that* really just happen? We were in way over our heads. And we had no idea how to dig our way out.

The stress took a toll on all of us. We each had strong opinions on what to do next, knowing that none of us were right. There was no "right." Nothing was black and white. It would have been simple if the children were healthy, but they were dying. The decision was one that would bring life or death. It felt like a thousand pounds on our chests.

When we got back to our room, we cried. We fought. We blamed one another. In the end, we knew it wasn't any of us who held the entire responsibility. We should have come more prepared. We thought we could just walk into a country and help kids in need, but it wasn't that simple. And we were finding that out the hard way.

◆ ◆ ◆

By the time the three of us headed back to the States

a few weeks later, we had taken in 18 children. There were a handful of children who tracked down their birth families. Those birth relatives fought the ministry to have their children removed from Ina's center and sent to us. We managed to also secure the special needs kids, because, honestly, Ina didn't want them. The ministry began sending us children in need of support. The rest were still stuck in the crossfire. We were exhausted and knew we had to get home to regroup and come up with a plan.

I packed up the rest of Adama's things, not knowing when or if I would ever see her again.

The grief growing inside me stayed buried for a while longer. I couldn't let it out yet. One tear shed for her would cause a tsunami. I buried her and allowed the guilt to rise inside of me instead.

19.

MODERN DAY MIRACLE
2010

What happens when people open their hearts? They get better.
—Haruki Murakami, *Norwegian Wood*

By the time we boarded the flight back to the States we had spent almost a month in Sierra Leone. I missed Jason so bad my insides literally hurt. I had walked so many roads and made so many decisions without him. We had been apart for so long. I just wanted to be home. And he was just that —home. As I sat in the row near the back of the plane, I closed my eyes and my mind began to wander to earlier that day.

◆ ◆ ◆

We had been asked to help with an intake at a nearby home. Supposedly there was little boy there in dire need. The staff estimated he was around eight years old. That's really all I knew about him. Honestly, I didn't want to go. I wanted to crawl in a hole and cry myself to sleep. I didn't want to see any more kids. I wanted to see Adama. That's who I wanted to see. But I pulled myself together and went anyway.

Thank God.

We pulled up to the house and a very old man was sitting outside on the porch. From the inside came a young woman. I assumed she was the birthmother. It turned out that she was the aunty. They sat down with us and told us their story. Her nephew, also the grandson of the old man, was the son of her older sister. She had died during childbirth and left little Sorie behind. His father had also died toward the end of the war. Both parents were gone, and they had so many other mouths to feed in the family they just couldn't continue caring for Sorie. I asked where the boy was so we could meet him. The grandfather pointed down the road with a big smile on his face. I could see a very small child making his way toward us. He looked so much younger than eight. His school uniform was tattered and way too big for him. His belt was wrapped twice around his waist and his toes were poking through his shoes. His legs were covered in scrapes and the bag he was carrying was almost as big as he was. As he approached, I could feel my heart slowly begin to open. The walls I had built were crumbling.

His smile felt electric. It pierced through me. It was sheepish and kind. This little boy seemed almost familiar to me. The more he smiled, the more his eyes would cut to the floor. He was so easily embarrassed. That's when it hit me. I saw Jordan in him. My own son. The smile was almost identical. I began thinking about Jordan and how much I missed him. How desperate I was to wrap him up inside my arms and never let him go. I had spent so much time away from him trying to save other children.

Voices cut through my thoughts, and I could hear them asking Sorie if he wanted to leave and come with us to the center to live. I expected him to cry and say no. Tears were streaming down the grandfather's face as they talked — another space in time where the world wasn't spinning quite right. It made more sense to keep this family together, but we didn't have the resources for that. We were asked to be part of a decision that, while in Sorie's best interest, felt so painfully wrong.

Sorie took very little time to decide. As soon as he was asked, he immediately said yes and quickly turned to grab his things. He was more than ready to go. I expected him to head inside the house, but he didn't. Instead he made his way down the ravine to the back of the home. Behind it was a small shack the size of a port-o-potty. He didn't live in the home at all. He lived out back. Alone in the shack.

This was devastating to me. I watched him as he did what grown children do. At only eight years old, he picked up and left home. He packed his sack. He changed his clothes. He put on his better pair of shoes, and then just walked away, never even looking back.

He climbed up into the car and sat on my lap. As we drove away his hands wrapped around mine, as though he was holding on for dear life. And at that moment it felt like he was saving me. Adama wasn't in my arms. Neither was Jordan. But Sorie was. I could see his face in the reflection on the glass, and he was still smiling. I knew in my gut this child was mine. I wouldn't dare speak it. But I knew. I knew he was my son. Further proof that, even in the dark, love finds its way to you. Even when our heart is breaking down, it still works when it needs to. I memorized the moment in the car, knowing I would have to tell Jason about him someday soon.

I just knew I loved him.

But I also loved Adama.

Since arriving back in the States, guilt had begun wrapping its fingers around me. Adama invaded my sleep. She sat in the back of mind, weighing down on me, finding her way into every thought. Mine always drifted back to her.

What was she doing? Was anyone holding her? Was the staff keeping up with her medicine? Was she being abused in the night like the other kids?

The answer was probably no to the first few questions and yes to the last. I have learned that, while orphanages might be better than the streets, there is also darkness there that is difficult to control. When hurting children fill rooms and hallways, and they are being cared for by hurting adults, well hurting people hurt people.

Our orphanage was no exception. We spent years hiring and firing to find the right mix of caregivers and staff to build the orphanage to where it is today. The early days were rough. The children came in scrappy and aggressive. Most had been in the streets or living in camps for a very long time. They had little to no education, and their main goal was to survive. Period. It didn't matter that they now had a bed, three solid meals a day, snacks, and a safe place to play. They couldn't just rewire their brains to feel safe. It didn't matter how hard we tried to convince them. These kids believed that at some point they would be forced back into the world they came from. So, they held their own, fought for their place, built walls around themselves, and it was up to us to tear them back down again.

Our center continued to grow a few children at a time. So many kids from so many different places. We had a six-year-old rock quarry laborer. An eight-year-old laundress. A baby boy who was left on the doorstep of our hotel. We had children who had come from the exploitation ring and children who had come from refugee camps. We had wanderers and street kids. We had special needs children and even teen moms. It was a circus. Chaos. A melting pot of pain. Yet a rainbow of hope at the same time. We were convinced we could bring healing to these kids. So, we continued to love, and to serve, and to do our best to protect them from themselves and from each other.

A few months after our doors were open, we got a startling call. There was a boating accident up-country in a village called Shenge, a community filled with a mostly Muslim population. Husbands had many wives and even more children. The community survived by farming. The men regularly loaded up boats with the harvest and all of the children who attended school each day. They would cross the water to a bigger city where the children would study, and the men would sell their goods. The women stayed behind in the village, keeping house and caring for the countless kids too young for school.

On this particular day, they overloaded the boat. This happened often. Usually they managed to make it across, but not on this day. On this day the Shenge community watched as the boat sunk, losing more than 200 men and children. The loss was a huge blow to the community. Losing the men of the home left women desperate for support. Many were left caring for ten or more children still left at home. It was a horrible tragedy. We were contacted by the government and asked if we had room to take in children. Reports stated there were little ones starving to death. Mothers were also starving and now faced the cruel reality of giving up their children to save them and themselves.

Osseh and the team from our center traveled to Shenge to assess how many kids we needed to bring back. We estimated we would bring in around six children. Not quite. We were a little off.

Osseh said the village was in one of the most desperate situations he had ever seen. The children had nothing. No clothes, no shoes, no food. They were wasting away. Their mothers were hollow-eyed and empty. After assessing the situation, the team felt there were at least 35 children who needed immediate placement and intervention.

What?

That more than doubled our numbers at the center. We barely had the children in the center sponsored as it was. We were down to the dime every month. The money was already spread so thin. It could take us a year to fully fund 35 more kids. I remember sitting in my car just crying. I was so scared. I knew we had to take them in, but I had no idea how we would feed them, let alone raise them all under one roof.

We decided to take them all in. All 35 of those children. Did we make a mistake? Maybe. All I know is that when children are dying, you look for the closest emergency room. Our center became that emergency room. We were not ready. We were not equipped. Our staff was not ready. Our storehouse was far from overflowing. But sometimes, you move anyway.

Sometimes you saddle up and take the damn mountain.

Thankfully a shipment of rice from Kids Against Hunger made its way across the world and into our storehouse right about the time the Shenge kids arrived. It felt like a miracle. Actually — it was a miracle. We had calculated the number of packets and determined we had enough food to last four to six months once the new kids arrived. That would buy us a little time to get the word out and raise more sponsorship support.

It was near Christmas and I was driving into Nashville when my phone rang. It was a staff member in Sierra Leone. He shared with me that the staff wanted to do something special for the community that holiday. They decide to host a community feeding program. They were planning to contribute enough meals to feed about 300 people.

I almost had a heart attack. I pulled off to the side of

the road. On one hand, I was so proud of the people working for us and so thankful they saw the needs around them and wanted to help. On the other hand, I was dying inside because we couldn't spare a single packet of rice. We needed every bit of it to hold us over till we raised enough sponsorship support. I did the math in my head and figured we needed about $10,000 to cover what the staff wanted to give away in the feeding program. Where on Earth would I get $10,000? I begged the staff not to go through with the program. Their silence told me they were shocked by my response and also that they were not going to budge.

Finally, I accepted the fact that we just gave away half the storehouse. I continued to sit on the side of the road, tears streaming down my face, begging God to help me figure this one out.

The next day I helped out a friend running a nonprofit. She was up and running but needed some organizational support. I offered to help out. Anything I could do to make extra money.

Toward the end of the day, my friend and I were sitting in the office chatting while she finished writing out my paycheck. She turned the page and started writing out another check. I assumed she had lots of people to pay that day. As I was gathering my things to leave, she reached out and handed me the second check.

Erica Stone

Erica, I feel led to donate something extra to the orphanage this month. I hope this will help you all as you continue working there.

It was folded in half as she handed it to me. I stuck it in my pocket, hugged her tight, thanked her, and wished her a happy holiday.

I got in my car and drove away. While I was sitting at a red light, I pulled the check out and opened it. I couldn't believe my eyes.

$10,000.

I found myself on the side of the road again, weeping. I could not believe it. A modern day miracle. This money protected our kids and would keep us up and running for six more months. We replaced every packet of rice we had given away. Not only were our children fed — so were 300 community members.

In Sierra Leone, you can't give out of excess because there is no excess. Every gift is given from a place of need, from a hand half empty — or half full, as our staff reminds us on a regular basis. Their hearts are so beautiful.

20.

2010

Never doubt a small group of thoughtful, committed citizens can change the world. It's the only thing that ever has.
—Margaret Meade

That first full year was so damn hard. Honestly, we had no clue what we were doing. It felt like it was one mistake after another. We were constantly underestimating the cost to operate. I have never been under such intense stress. We knew we needed people to grasp the vision, although we were still trying to figure out exactly what that vision was. We had created a stop-gap, but we needed to decide what we wanted to do long term. Our work couldn't begin and end with an orphanage. The kids deserved more than that. We knew we had to get feet on the ground. We needed eyes opened and hearts as wrecked as ours were. We needed an army to help us continue forward.

We sent our first official mission team in 2010. I brought Jordan on the trip. I felt it was important for him to see with his own eyes the reason his mom was gone so much. He needed a picture in his mind that explained the nights I spent pacing the floors and the days I spent in bed, unable to function. He needed to know why. He needed to know why Adama wasn't home yet. He was young but not too young to be exposed to the realities of the world. It was time he got a front-row seat to the country that had taken over our entire life.

It was a beautiful trip. The team members were lovely human beings with capable hearts, interested only in serving and understanding the culture they were so privileged to visit. Jordan was a trooper. He and his little cousin Malachi served their hearts out. I knew then that one day he would understand why we had sacrificed so much, and he would know it had been the right thing.

During those first trips many got sick. We dealt with typhoid fever and malaria often in the early days. Our guest quarters were not always the safest places in town to stay, but we were always on a budget. We worked with the hand we were dealt.

2010 ended up being a big year for us, not only in Sierra Leone but personally as well.

We filled capacity at the center and moved to a larger compound later that year. We were now caring for more than 100 children. We had more than 50 staff members. We had employed pastors, caregivers, laundry workers, cleaners, teachers, security, cooks, the list goes on and on. It takes a village to raise 100 kids. If we had had the space that number would have been significantly higher. And there were times it was. It was hard to say no when a child was brought to us. Yet we knew we had to start setting policies and standards for admission and care. That was the year we grew from infancy to what felt like the teen years all in one night. We knew we couldn't operate with all heart, yet how badly we wanted to. When hardship surrounds you all the time, it's so hard to turn your back. But we had 100+ kids inside our walls and they needed us to step up our game. So we did. We brought in therapeutic support, raised our level of medical care, and focused on education. We were constantly working and planning and learning everything the hard way.

Personally, Jason and I had fallen in love with three children at the center. By this time, he knew all about Sorie, but it was on one of Jason's trips to Sierra Leone that Capri and Nash entered our orbit, crashing into us and changing our life footprint, yet again. Capri stuck to Jason like glue that trip, and he was smitten.

He would call me and talk all about her little red dress and her high-pitched singing voice. I told him she had a brother. Jason's response: The more the merrier. Let's adopt all of them.

So, we made more room in our hearts. It wasn't hard. I've come to realize our hearts are made for stretching. There is always room to love more. The loving part is the greatest lesson I've learned these last 15 years. The loving just never stops. We sometimes want to run from it, but we can't out run it. It always finds us somehow and dares us to show up again.

The adoption ban was still in place, so we continued to fight it. We now had four children on the line that we had to get home. So many others felt called to adopt. Homes were waiting, forever families, but we needed a path.

As the years passed news spread about our work in Sierra Leone, and the number of teams we sent in quadrupled. There were years we sent close to 200 people to serve. The trips were meant to open eyes, open hearts, and, honestly, also to open pocket books. There is no pretending that a 24/7 facility doesn't need a constant flow of cash, especially as we continued to grow. Sending volunteer teams was an absolute necessity.

So many women seemed to find a purpose in Sierra Leone that extended beyond their life back in the States. I think when mothers arrive in a world where so many are motherless, there is no option but to wrap your arms around every kid you can and just love them for as long as you can.

We may have sent six teams or more to Sierra Leone when we deiced to start including more and more community work. We obviously wanted the teams to get to know the children and work inside our walls. We also felt it was critical they spend time in the hospitals and in the communities to understand where our kids came from and what they survived.

On one particular trip we came up with the idea to operate a feeding program for one of the poorest areas of Freetown, Kroo Bay. It was a slum that had settled on a giant trash dump, with more than 15,000 people living there. It was situated right inside the bay. Freetown is nestled into a large mountain so you can imagine the trash that flows down the mountain and into the bay every day. It may very well be one of the worst places on the planet. An estimated 4,000 orphans live there. You can drive through the area and watch the children, naked, bathing in and looking for food in the sewer. The smell could knock you out. It was not uncommon to see dead animals floating in the water, right next to the children as they bathed and played.

We had operated many feeding programs in the past and they all went very well. We never stopped to consider what a feeding day would actually look like in an area this desperate.

We showed up early and set up shop inside a building in the center of the dump. We brought all of our center cooks and senior staff with us. We told the community leaders we were there to feed the children. We would cook enough meals to feed about 500 kids. It would be up to the community leaders to invite who they felt should come. We couldn't allow adults; we simply didn't have enough food. We were there specifically for the orphaned kids. We asked the leaders to control the outer perimeter and to help navigate the lines as they formed. We brought in 50 children at a time, sat them down, fed them and then brought a new group in. We knew the children had to eat inside. If they left with the food, it would be stolen from them.

Everything started out fine, but word spread quickly throughout the village that hot meals were being given away. Before we knew it, we had thousands of people pressing in. We were basically locked inside. We couldn't get in or out. We got rushed by the crowd every time we opened the doors to welcome in a new group. The numbers continued to grow. We continued to cook for as long as we could and then eventually just started bagging rice and handing it off.

I'm not sure how it happened except to say it was another moment that can only be explained as a miracle. We somehow ended up feeding thousands of people that day, not 500. Children and adults. How the food lasted, only God can explain that. When we ran out, things got ugly. The crowds wouldn't let up, and we were forced to evacuate the premises. We had to be escorted to the vehicles.

There were many tears that day. Not because we had fed so many, but because we didn't get the chance to spend time with anyone. We just wanted to give and love on as many people as we could. But we ended up running from them in the end. What happened to being united as one and refusing to draw a line between "us" and "them?" It wasn't the outreach we hoped it would be. It turned dangerous for the team in the end, and we couldn't take risks like that, at least not with inexperienced travelers. That was painful.

We learned a very valuable lesson. While it's important to help the very neediest of people, sometimes that desperation makes people do desperate things and you find yourself in an unsafe environment. We could not fix the hungry with one meal. Honestly, what the hell were we thinking? We were intent on "making a difference," even a small one, without understanding these people didn't need a band-aid or a hand out. They needed way more than that. They needed bulldozers and construction crews. They needed medical care and a clean water supply. Did we have the answers? No. So how do we fix it? I honestly still don't know.

I wish I did.

21.

THE RESURRECTION
2011

> *It is impossible for you to go on as you were before, so you must go on as you never have.*
> —Cheryl Strayed, *Tiny Beautiful Things*

Well here we are. We've come full circle. Smack dab in the middle of 2011. The year she died. The year I died as well inside.

I wish I could say that eight years later I've reconciled it all, that I've come to peace with the why, why it all happened. I wish I could say that I've learned a life lesson that will move and reshape your heart like it did mine. But I'm not sure I can.

What I do know is that 2011 will forever be the year I lost my whole world and then gained it all back, but differently.

I was in and out of the country more times that I can remember. While I battled the adoption law, making our presence known in every government office, Adama was living her last few months on this Earth. She was right under my nose, within arm's reach during each visit, yet she might as well have been 100,000 miles away.

With every other journey, and in almost every story since, there was always a bend in the road for me. A moment when the tide would turn and our luck would change. When the God who holds this universe as I've always believed moved his hand and we were given what we'd prayed for. Love, life, forgiveness, hope. Maybe another chance.

But not this time. At least not in the way I had planned. But isn't that exactly how life works sometimes? I believe we make choices. Those choices determine the turns in the road. For me, and for Adama, my choice caused a bridge to wash out. The end of our journey was abrupt and swift. The road came to an end, and there was no crossing to the other side.

Our time together was done.

The weeks and months after her death carried on slow and steady. You see, time doesn't stop for death or grief. We are forced to move on. I spent weeks in bed after Adama died. Replaying the burial, trying desperately to feel her fingers in mine. I stayed in bed because, there, I could keep my eyes closed, and just remember her.

My whole world came apart that year. But, at the same exact time, in the same exact month, in the same exact week, another baby was born. As Adama lay in the ground, another child was brought into the world. While I was bent over Adama's grave, a guilt-filled mother mourning the loss of her daughter, there was another baby girl on the other side of the city. Her mother died while giving birth to her. Eight months after she was born, I found this little girl.

During the eight months following Adama's death, I slept mostly. I forgot about my love for the music business, put my work on the shelf, and simply functioned as best I could. When I wasn't fighting depression, I was advocating for adoption with more aggression than ever before. My nature changed. My personality shifted. I was on a mission. I couldn't live with Adama being just another statistic. Her death catapulted me into action. I spoke from pulpits. I stood in front of the highest government officials in Sierra Leone, pushing for adoption reform, hoping that every step I took would somehow make her count. Adama was in the ground because there was too much gray in the fabric of the adoption process. The laws were not upheld. The rights of the child were never considered, and tribal ties always trumped the law.

That needed to change. I couldn't bear the thought of ever having another child buried while a family was waiting for that child to come home. There was a world of wrong in Sierra Leone that somehow needed to be made right. Was it my fight?

You're damn right it was.

I can remember the spring trip in 2012. I took Jayda back to Sierra Leone. Partly because she was ready to meet her birth family and partly because I had a plan. I wanted to take her back to all of the government offices that played a role in her adoption. I wanted to introduce her to all of the people who either stood in our way or made a way, hoping that when they took one look at her they would understand the ban must be lifted. Jayda was an example of what adoption could look like when done legally and authentically.

It was an amazing trip. It was my first time back since Adama's death. Jayda and I visited the grave where her sister was buried. After being there and then meeting her relatives, she came face to face with what truly made her an orphan. It wasn't just an unemployed mother. It wasn't just poverty. It wasn't just the death of a parent. It was all of that and so much more. It was a country unable to support its people. It was a war that caused that country to crumble, leaving so many like her in its wake. Rebuilding takes time. Sometimes you won't see the rebuild for at least a generation. Jayda saw with her own eyes that nothing could have prevented her from becoming an orphan.

That was life for children in Sierra Leone.

Her visits to the high court and to the other government officials did exactly what we hoped it would do. They were floored by her appearance. They were shocked by how much she had grown. They paraded her around like a celebrity.

After many more months of advocating, the ban finally lifted. I couldn't have been more excited. This meant that Sorie, Nash, and Capri would soon come home. My heart ached that the ban didn't happen sooner for Adama's sake.

That same year, on another trip, I went into a very small community with the team to do some work. It was on that day that I had an encounter with a very pregnant woman, carrying a very malnourished baby on her back. The child looked so similar to Adama when I first found her, I almost fell over. I couldn't stop staring at her. I watched as the woman stood in line waiting for food support. My heart bled for her. It was clear the baby on her back was dying. How would she ever support the next one she was about to give birth to? It turned out, the child on her back wasn't hers. She was a baby whose mama died during childbirth eight months earlier. We took her in and, thankfully, the little one began to thrive.

I took photos of her every time I visited Sierra Leone

in hopes of finding her a family. After our adoptions went through and the kids came home I made it my mission to advocate for this little one. I couldn't find a soul to take interest in her. It was so strange. Most of the time it was hard to find families for the older kids. Younger ones, especially babies, would get snatched up quicker than anyone. I couldn't understand why she was so hard to match.

Jason traveled back to Sierra Leone a few months later. He called me one day from the center and he was choked up, telling me the story of a little baby girl he had fallen in love with. It made my skin crawl. I didn't want another little girl. I wanted Adama. We had just brought home all of our kids. Our life was chaos. But he wouldn't let up. I could tell in his voice he was head over heels in love with this little girl.

I called a friend who was on the team with Jason and asked her to pull the little girl's file. I needed to find out who she was. She was the same little one I had been advocating for. And you will never believe it — her birth certificate stated she was born at the exact same time I was in-country burying Adama.

I lost my world and gained it back.

Willa came home only a few short months after Jason first called me from the center to tell me about her. The decision to adopt her was hard and easy all at the same time. I knew without a doubt Willa was meant for us. It was the universe's way of giving us back what had been taken from us. But, oddly, I didn't want it. I needed to stay in the dark and continue to mourn. I couldn't let myself love her. But love pursues us. Just when we think we have nothing left to give, we find the space to love again. But maybe differently this time.

Willa was a wrecking ball. She took my broken heart, broke it down even further, and then she rebuilt me. She became my new world.

And that world looked different.

22.

HOMECOMING
2013

There's no place like home.
—Dorothy, *The Wizard of Oz*

With the adoption ban gone, it was like the flood gates had opened. We had spent so much time in the trenches, leading up to this moment. All of the fraud we had experienced in Jayda's adoption, the years of toiling for Adama, the years of legal study to learn how to advocate for better interpretation of the laws had finally paid off. We spent so much time working and perfecting an adoption process that would be foolproof, creating a paper trail that could be modeled by other agencies and centers. We couldn't help but feel proud of how far we had come.

Case by case, family by family, children came home. It was beautiful to watch it all unfold. We were among those families. We had spent so much time with them all. Some of us moms spent months in-country, fighting for our kids together and trying to get through a process that didn't really exist. We never wavered, and we forged a path that lit the way for all who would come after us. If only those adopting today knew and understood the sacrifices of the mothers who came before them. If only they realized how many faced loss after loss after loss, so that one day others would have a win.

When you're in the thick of the adoption journey, you are prepared for the wait. You are warned that things don't always go the way they should, and that red tape is something we cannot always maneuver. You are not always taught about what to expect when the children actually do come home. Not everyone is prepared for the fall-out. Oh yes, you didn't know? There is absolutely a fall-out. It's the moment you realize you may have just made the biggest mistake of your life. The moment you thought you had it in you but now you're not so sure. The moment you are standing in the hallway staring at the children who are supposed to love you back as much as you love them, and you realize they don't. They don't love you at all. Or maybe you don't love them as much as you thought you did. You begin to understand that adoption is like a marriage. It's work. You come to the realization that adoption is also a process. It's a love that sometimes feels conditional. You have to decide to love these children even when you don't want to. You have to be the grown up. It's a relationship that you feel ill equipped for. It's a road that stays dark, sometimes for years at a time. You wait and love and pray for the child to somehow heal.

Kids don't just fit into families. Families are not boxes we place new children inside of and expect it to just all play out like the perfect gift we claim it to be. They are not puzzle pieces. If we find they don't quite "fit" we don't just throw them out. We can't just change our minds.

Adoption is messy. Just like love. It hurts. We bleed out. We find ourselves tending to wounds far more often than we want to admit. Children leave scars where they cut us, and we leave just as many when we fail them too.

Adopted children are not statistics. They are not areas of service. They are human beings with heart and soul and an ocean of pain they are trying not to drown in.

We are supposed to be the lifeboat, the captain of a ship intent on rescuing them. But we can't. Some children learn to swim, some reach for the life vest; others don't.

We want to be the answer. We want to fix it all. Sometimes the truth smacks you in the face and you realize maybe it isn't the child who has a problem. Maybe it's you. You start to wake up and understand that sometimes we step into the world of orphan care thinking we're doing the rescuing, yet, all the while, it was us who needed to be rescued. We needed to be reminded that the world does not begin and end with us. There is more. We are wearing skin and bone that is rooted in purpose. We are meant to be stretched, broken, and then stitched back up again.

I thought about sharing a few stories of my own kids. What our mission field has looked like at home. I could tell you of battles we have fought, trauma we have had to endure. But I've decided to let that lie. After all, it isn't my story. Those stories belong to my children. I do believe one day they will use their voices and tell them, owning their truth and proving love can rebuild the most battered heart.

I think the greatest lesson I've learned from my children is that love never gives up.

Ever.

23.

THE AFTERLIFE
PRESENT

I had no idea history was being made. I was just tired of giving up.
—Rosa Parks

When we think of the afterlife we always think about it in terms of what happens to us after we die. Where do we go after our bodies are placed in the ground? Is there life after death? Most of us think we know the answer to these questions yet the world continues to ask. After all, until you die, how can you really know for sure?

For me, I sometimes think of the afterlife in terms of this life.

After the fact.
After the breakdown.
After the break-up.
After the illness.
After the betrayal.
After the loss.
After the death.

What do we do with the life we are forced to begin again?

I think about my life in two parts: Before Adama died and after. She is that pivotal moment for me. It wasn't high school graduation or college. It wasn't a wedding or becoming a mother. Of course those moments were important, but the monumental moment that changed everything for me forever was her.

I knew at some point I would get to this part right here. The part where I would somehow have to wrap this whole thing up. Where I would finally be forced to place a period in the last chapter of her story.

But the thing is, she just goes on and on.

And I am so glad for that.

Who I was before Adama — and who I am today because of her — are two very different women.

Loving her made me crazy and difficult to live with. Loving her made me walk a road called depression, forcing me to understand it and have so much compassion for those living in that space.

Loving her made me question legality vs. morality. Adama taught me that sometimes the right and moral choice isn't legal, and the legal choice isn't always moral. Loving her made me walk away from legalism and judgment and embrace humanity in ways I couldn't do before I knew her. She helped me understand that sometimes it's okay to do the unthinkable when it results in the right thing.

She put a fire in my bones that will never go out. She is why I believe in Sierra Leone. She is why I believe so much good exists there.

Adama is why I build things. She is why I refuse to give in or give up. She is why I will always go back, even when I want to run. She is why I no longer take no for an answer.

The choice I made when walking away from her made me very self-aware that we are sometimes very ugly inside. We are held responsible for every decision we make. There are no excuses. Sometimes we don't get a second chance. So, we better get it right the first time.

Sometimes when I go to the beach with my family, I imagine what it would be like to have her in the family photographs. She would be 10 years old today, as I write this. I'm sure she would be as feisty as my other girls. But I also wonder what would make her unique. Would she have played the violin or been a gymnast? Would she have been independent in nature or like to snuggle? I wonder what her laugh would sound like. Would she be a jokester like her dad or super serious like me? I don't know. But sometimes I like to imagine what she may have been like. I like to imagine her arms wrapped around me and mine around her, what it would have been like if I'd never let her go.

I know that the guilt I carry is heavy. Too heavy. I'd love to lay it down and leave it all behind. My friends tell me that I had no choice that day. They say Adama wouldn't want me living this way. I know they are probably right.

Yet I still carry that guilt. I always will. After years of therapy, I am finally learning to have grace for myself. I'm learning I did the best I could with the information I had then. That has to be enough, though I will likely wrestle with this always.

And that's okay.

In terms of the center, the afterlife has been a whirlwind. We eventually got all of the special needs children from Ina's center transferred to us, and every single one has been adopted and is now in the States. The rest of the children are still inside the gates. Ina was never shut down, and I doubt she ever will be.

The man who demanded the bribe — $10,000 per child — was eventually killed in a car accident. I'm not sure how I feel about that. I've been told there are centers just like Ina's all over the coast of West Africa, and so the vicious cycle of injustice continues.

We have seen more than 200 children come through our doors. Close to 70 have been adopted, and many more are waiting to be united with families.

Our staff is incredible. They have poured their lives into that place, even going so far as adopting children themselves. This opened our eyes to the fact that we needed to expand our vision and provide stability for children who would stay in Sierra Leone after they are grown. We now encourage in-country adoptions and run a ROOTS house for older children transitioning from center life to community life.

We continue to build. We continue to learn. We continue to hope that, because of the village of people supporting us throughout the years, the children we've all raised will one day raise their nation. I firmly believe one day these children we have all come to love will end the cycles of oppression and will become the change we are all waiting and hoping for. Will we see it happen in our lifetime? I sure hope so.

In some ways I believe Adama is and will always be the heartbeat of the orphanage. I know her memory has settled into the bones of all who worked so hard to protect her. I know she is why Osseh never stops. I know she is why none of us will ever stop trying.

Erica Stone

Adama,

You will be the reason we continue to advocate for every child like you who lives without a voice. For every child like you who didn't get the chance to grow up. May this story, your story, be the catalyst. And may your spirit live on in everything we do. For always.

I love you my sweet, sweet girl.

POSTFACE

Emmanuel

I'm sure you remember the incredible miracle that occurred the day I found Emmanuel — the brother we never knew Jayda had. You may wonder what happened to him and how he fits into our lives now. Sadly, I often wonder the same thing.

Sometimes your world collides with someone else, like ours did with Emmanuel. I like to call it a divine appointment, a collision that was meant to be for so many reasons. When you realize someone needs you because he's lost hope, you do everything in your power to help him begin again, especially when you realize what he's been through. You know that with just a little bit of support, an entire life can turn around. What we don't always take into account is the pain people carry on their backs, the past that controls their future and holds them for ransom. It's a cost that, in the end, no one can pay but the individual. Eventually, they have to decide to trade the past for a future. But for many, pain becomes comfortable, almost like a safety blanket. They'd rather stay covered by that pain than find a way to dig out from underneath it. They are just too tired to dig. Too broken. Too scarred. So they settle into the pain and refuse to leave it behind.

That was Emmanuel.

After finding him, Emmanuel quickly became part of our family. He was too old to be adopted, but we did everything in our power to help him understand he would never be alone again. I do know he believed us. At least he wanted to. We paid for his schooling and also for housing. We wanted to get him out from under Ina's thumb as quickly as possible. We secured him an apartment, paid his school fees, made sure he had food and all the other necessities to become a self-sufficient young adult. We also gave him a job at the orphanage. He was a very hard worker, fit right in, and he seemed to carry hope in his pocket and a dream in his heart.

For a season, everything went well.

I thought the positive steps forward would be enough to catapult him into his future. They weren't. Eventually, things began to shift. Emmanuel started to slip through our fingers. To this day I'm not sure why. He began missing work and missing classes. I had feared he was falling back into a "street life" or a "survivalist" mentality. Many people who struggle for most of their lives can't see or focus on what comes next. They can't see past their needs for the day. They don't know how to think about the future. They have never lived with that privilege. They don't know how to plan. Even worse, they don't know how to hope. They only know how to endure.

Emmanuel only knew how to move from one day to the next. He didn't understand that if he missed work, he wouldn't get paid. If he continued to miss class, he wouldn't graduate. So when times got tough, he reverted back to just surviving rather than thriving.

He gave up.

He would go missing for weeks at a time. We would hear nothing from him. Then he would show back up again. Osseh would have long talks with him, trying to encourage him to stick to the path, but eventually Emmanuel lost sight of where his hope was. He returned to his former way of life, one where struggle came naturally and his only goal was the immediate. What he would eat and where he would sleep.

Tomorrow? Well, that's tomorrow.

In his mind, there was no guarantee tomorrow would come.

It's rare we see him these days, and it's one of the saddest things we have faced while on this journey. I think about him all the time. I often wonder if he's found hope in something and pray he finds joy somewhere in his life. After all, he deserves the world. He had a smile that shook my insides, just like Jayda's smile does. He had a heart bigger than most and was a critical part in helping expose injustice. He was quite the fighter.

I have to believe that one day he will remember who he is and that he is capable of breaking the cycle he was raised in. And one day, if and when he remembers, we will be there with arms wide open, loving him as we always have.

Family.

Love.

The fight to pursue both is a constant battle.

I suppose that's because we all live a bit broken and we all bleed out sometimes. It's the gathering up of the pieces and the putting back together part that truly defines who we are and where love resides. I'm finding it's in all of us, rebuilding our hearts, one day at a time.

One day Emmanuel will find his way back to us.

After all, love always does.

A Special Thanks

I wouldn't have finished this book were it not for the community of hearts protecting and surrounding me during the time it took - to put pen to paper.

To the "favorite's thread". Thank you for protecting and defending my heart during some of my darkest days. Your loyalty is unmatched.

To every church, every community group, and all the other lovely humans I've encountered along the way that choose love above all else. Thank you for stepping into the trenches with me, when turning your head and looking away would have been so much easier.

To the SL judges, attorneys, and ministry staff that have stood with us on behalf of the orphan. It is because of you that children in Sierra Leone have hope again.

To the TRS staff in Sierra Leone. I love you. You teach me to love deeper, fight harder, and to give more than I ever thought possible.

To Wes. Thank you for your patience while I found my way back to myself. Now let's finally do this thing.

To Greg and Rebecca. Thank you for taking such great care of this story... in more ways than one.

To Aubrey. Thank you for being my fierce defender and confidant. I love you sister.

*To Fran. Thank you for carrying on the dream in Sierra Leone.
I believe in you. Always.*

Made in the USA
Lexington, KY
22 March 2019